Monographs in Aerospace History #10

NASA's Origins and the Dawn of the Space Age

by David S.F. Portree

NASA History Division
Office of Policy and Plans
NASA Headquarters
Washington, DC 20546

September 1998

Foreword

When future generations review the history of the twentieth century, they will undoubtedly judge humanity's movement into space, with both machines and people, as one of its seminal developments. Even at this juncture, the compelling nature of spaceflight—and the activity that it has engendered on the part of many peoples and governments—makes the U.S. civil space program a significant area of investigation. People from all avenues of experience and levels of education share an interest in the drama of spaceflight.

This monograph relates for a general audience the origins of the space age, the creation of the National Aeronautics and Space Administration (NASA), and the first tentative steps toward an operational capability to undertake space exploration. To a very real extent, NASA emerged in 1958 out of the "cold war" rivalries of the United States and the Soviet Union, which were engaged in a broad battle over the ideologies and allegiances of the nonaligned nations of the world. Space exploration was one major area contested. The Soviets gained the upper hand in this competition on October 4, 1957, when they launched Sputnik I, the first artificial satellite to orbit Earth, as part of a larger scientific effort associated with the International Geophysical Year.

While U.S. officials congratulated the Soviet Union for this accomplishment, clearly many Americans thought that the Soviet Union had staged a tremendous coup for the communist system at U.S. expense. Because of this perception, Congress passed and President Dwight D. Eisenhower signed the National Aeronautics and Space Act of 1958, establishing the new agency with a broad mandate to explore and use space for the benefit "of all mankind." NASA began operations on October 1, 1958, absorbing into it the earlier National Advisory Committee for Aeronautics intact—its 8,000 employees, an annual budget of $100 million, three major research laboratories (Langley Aeronautical Laboratory, Ames Aeronautical Laboratory, and Lewis Flight Propulsion Laboratory), and two small test facilities. NASA soon added other facilities.

NASA began to conduct space missions within months of its creation, especially Project Mercury to ascertain the possibilities of human spaceflight. Even so, these activities were constrained by a modest budget and a measured pace on the part of NASA leadership. That changed rather suddenly on May 25, 1961, when President John F. Kennedy, responding to perceived challenges to U.S. leadership in science and technology, announced a lunar landing effort that would place an American on the Moon before the end of the decade.

This monograph relates the story of those early years and reprints facsimile copies of key documents. At the time of the NASA's fortieth anniversary, it seems fitting to revisit its origins and to reflect on its accomplishments since.

This is the tenth in a series of monographs prepared under the auspices of the NASA History Division. The **Monographs in Aerospace History** series is designed to provide a wide variety of investigations relative to the history of aeronautics and space. These publications are intended to be tightly focused in terms of subject, relatively short in length, and reproduced in an inexpensive format to allow for timely and broad dissemination to researchers in aerospace history. Suggestions for additional publications in the **Monographs in Aerospace History** series are welcome.

Roger D. Launius
Chief Historian
National Aeronautics and Space Administration
July 1, 1998

Table of Contents

Sputnik Night: October 4–5, 1958 1

Korolev and Freedom of Space: February 14, 1955–October 4, 1957 1

One Small Ball in the Air: October 4, 1957–November 3, 1957 5

The Birth of NASA: November 3, 1957–October 1, 1958 7

Denouement—NASA's First Eighteen Months: 12
October 1, 1958–December 20, 1960

Notes 14

Key Events 17

Documents 19

   Document 1 19
   United States Information Agency, "World Opinion and the Soviet Satellite: A
   Preliminary Evaluation," October 17, 1957

   Document 2 27
   James R. Killian, Jr., "Memorandum on Organizational Alternatives for Space
   Research and Development," December 30, 1957

   Document 3 35
   L.A. Minnich, Jr., "Legislative Leadership Meeting, Supplementary Notes,"
   February 4, 1958

   Document 4 41
   S. Paul Johnston, Memorandum for Dr. J. R. Killian, Jr., "Activities," February 21,
   1958, with attached: Memorandum for Dr. J. R. Killian, Jr., "Preliminary Observations
   on the Organization for the Exploitation of Outer Space," February 21, 1958

   Document 5 53
   James R. Killian, Jr., Special Assistant for Science and Technology; Percival Brundage,
   Director, Bureau of the Budget; and Nelson A. Rockefeller, Chairman, President's
   Advisory Committee on Government Organization, Memorandum for the President,
   "Organization for Civil Space Programs," March 5, 1958, with attached: "Summary
   of Advantages and Disadvantages of Alternative Organizational Arrangements"

   Document 6 73
   The President's Science Advisory Committee, "Introduction to Outer Space,"
   March 26, 1958

   Document 7 85
   "Main Problems in the Senate Bill Establishing a Federal Space Agency," July 7, 1958

   Document 8 91
   "National Aeronautics and Space Act of 1958," Public Law 85–568, 72 Stat. 426,
   signed by President Eisenhower on July 29, 1958

   Document 9 107
   Special Committee on Space Technology, "Recommendations to the NASA Regarding
   a National Civil Space Program," October 28, 1958

NASA's Origins and the Dawn of the Space Age

Sputnik Night: October 4–5, 1957

The world's first artificial satellite, Sputnik, lifted off from Soviet Central Asia at 10:26 p.m. Moscow time on Friday, October 4, 1957. At 1:22 a.m. the next morning, Radio Moscow announced that Earth had a new, Soviet-made moon. By then the 83.6-kilogram (184.3-pound) aluminum alloy sphere had twice passed unnoticed over the United States, where it was then mid-afternoon on October 4.

One of the first Americans to learn of the launch was Dr. Lloyd Berkner, the geophysicist who, in 1950, had suggested that the time was ripe for an international program of global geophysical research. Berkner's suggestion grew into the eighteen-month International Geophysical Year (IGY) of 1957–58.[1] He soon became coordinator for IGY rocket and satellite plans.

At about 6:15 p.m. U.S. Eastern time on October 4, 1957, Berkner was at the Soviet Embassy in Washington, D.C., for a reception wrapping up the week-long IGY Rockets and Satellites Conference. The news from Moscow came by telephone to Walter Sullivan, senior science correspondent for the *New York Times*, and made its way to Berkner, who called for quiet and announced: "I have just been informed by the *New York Times* that a Russian satellite is in orbit at an elevation of 900 kilometers. I wish to congratulate our Soviet colleagues on their achievement."[2]

Half a world away, in Barcelona, Spain, many delegates to the 8th International Astronautical Congress had gone to their hotel rooms, after a busy day of presentations, by the time the news broke. Some, such as British author Arthur C. Clarke, first learned of Sputnik when they were awakened by reporters seeking authoritative comment on the Soviet achievement.[3] The aerospace industry magazine *Aviation Week* reported that the Barcelona Congress became an impromptu international forum for "much animated informal discussion about what the U.S. could do to recoup some of its scientific prestige. Manned space flight or hitting the moon were the two most common suggestions, but even those were tinged with doubt that there still existed an American lead in these categories." The magazine quoted an unnamed U.S. military official at the Congress as saying, "if it weighs 18 pounds they're ahead of us—if it weighs 180 pounds, I'm scared!" An unnamed European delegate, the magazine also reported, pointed to the twenty-three U.S. and five Soviet papers at the Congress and pointedly concluded that "Americans talk about [spaceflight] and the Russians do it."[4]

Over the next few weeks, the Sputnik launch emerged as a watershed in the history of the cold war. The twelve-month period beginning with Sputnik's launch ended with the birth of the U.S. civilian space agency, the National Aeronautics and Space Administration (NASA). The agency's creation was a product of post-Sputnik fears, but it was shaped also by cautious Eisenhower administration space policies established in the early 1950s, soon after launching a satellite first emerged as a serious possibility.

Korolev and Freedom of Space: February 14, 1955–October 4, 1957

The space programs of the cold war adversaries formed a symbiotic relationship—a race in which each competitor spurred the other forward—several years before Sputnik. With the collapse of the Soviet Union in 1991, much new information on the prehistory of the Soviet space program became available.[5]

President Dwight D. Eisenhower meets with Harold Stasson, a special assistant who was largely responsible for drafting the "Open Skies" proposal, in the Oval Office on March 22, 1955.

MONOGRAPHS IN AEROSPACE HISTORY #10

One man dominated Soviet space engineering in the 1950s and 1960s. Sergei Pavlovich Korolev headed a Soviet amateur rocketry organization in the 1930s and survived Joseph Stalin's forced labor camps to build missiles in the 1940s and 1950s. On May 20, 1954, the Soviet government ordered Korolev's design bureau, OKB-1, to develop the first Soviet intercontinental ballistic missile (ICBM), the R-7. On May 26, Korolev dispatched to the Soviet government the *Report on an Artificial Satellite of the Earth*, authored by his old friend Mikhail Klavdiyevich Tikhonravov. He pointed out that the R-7 missile could be used as a satellite launcher and included written materials from the United States that demonstrated American interest in satellite launches.[6]

Work toward U.S. satellites occurred on several levels in the early 1950s. Civilian interest centered on the possibility of launching science satellites during the IGY. At the same time, the military carried out several reconnaissance satellite studies. The major issue affecting the timing of subsequent U.S. satellite launches apparently emerged as early as June 1952 in the "Beacon Hill Report," authored by a fifteen-person study group convening at Massachusetts Institute of Technology. The report pointed out that military satellites would orbit over Soviet territory and could thus be considered a violation of national sovereignty. For this reason, the report stated, their deployment would have to be authorized at the U.S. presidential level.[7]

On February 14, 1955, the Technological Capabilities Panel ("the Surprise Attack Panel") issued its report, *Meeting the Threat of Surprise Attack*, in which it reiterated the Beacon Hill group's contention and suggested a solution. The panel advised that a small science satellite should be launched as early as possible to establish the principle of "freedom of space" for military satellites that would follow.[8] President Eisenhower's advisers adopted the principle of "freedom of space" soon thereafter.[9]

By this time, the discussion of a science satellite was well advanced in U.S. scientific circles. This culminated in a U.S.-sponsored initiative prompting the international ruling body of the IGY to call for science satellite launches during the IGY. The resolution was adopted in Rome on October 4, 1954.

The Rome resolution pulled back the hammer on the starter's gun in the satellite race. It helped ensure that Korolev's preliminary satellite work did not languish, and it led to the creation of the Interdepartmental Commission for the Coordination and Control of Work in the Field of Organization and Accomplishment of Interplanetary Communications, the first organization within the Soviet Academy of Sciences devoted to spaceflight.[10] This organization, the existence of which was announced on April 16, 1955, was chaired by Academician Leonid Sedov.

The announcement of plans for the building and launching of the world's first artificial satellite on July 29, 1955. Presidential press secretary James Hagerty is shown with five scientists during the meeting at which the announcement of President Eisenhower's approval of the plan was made. Front, left to right: Dr. Alan T. Waterman, Hagerty, Dr. S. Douglas Cornell, and Dr. Alan Shapley. Standing, left to right: Dr. J. Wallace Joyce and Dr. Athelstan Spilhaus.

A month before Sedov's announcement, on March 14, 1955, the U.S. National Committee for the IGY had issued a report declaring feasible a U.S. science satellite launch during the IGY. It submitted the report to the National Science Foundation, which took it to President Eisenhower. On May 18, 1955, the U.S. IGY committee formally approved the satellite project. The National Security Council (NSC) considered the project on May 20, 1955, and issued a draft policy statement (NSC 5520). On May 26, 1955, the NSC formally approved U.S. government participation in the U.S. IGY science satellite project. The NSC's unstated aims were to establish the principle of "freedom of space" and to accrue for the United States the prestige benefits of launching the first satellite. The IGY science satellite program was not to interfere with high-priority missile programs.[11] On May 27, Eisenhower approved the plan. On July 29, 1955, Eisenhower's press secretary, James Hagerty, announced that the United States would launch a science satellite during the IGY.

Without realizing it, Eisenhower fired the starter's gun in the race to launch an Earth satellite. News of the announcement reached the 6th International Astronautical Congress in Copenhagen, Denmark, on August 2, 1955, where Academician Sedov was in attendance. That same day, Sedov held a press conference at the Soviet Embassy in Copenhagen, at which he announced that "the realization of the [Soviet] satellite project can be expected in the near future."[12]

On August 30, 1955, Korolev presented to the Soviet government's Military-Industrial Commission a new satellite report completed two weeks earlier by Tikhonravov. On the basis of the report, the commission approved using the R-7 ICBM to launch a one-and-a-half-ton satellite—this over opposition from Soviet missile specialists, who worried that the satellite effort would interfere with ballistic missile development. Later that day, Korolev told representatives of the Soviet Academy of Sciences that he could launch the first in a series of IGY science satellites in April–June 1957, before the IGY started. The Academy representatives approved the project. Work on the satellite's scientific program began immediately, but the Soviet Council of Ministers did not issue its formal decree authorizing the program (No. 149-88ss) until January 30, 1956.[13] The satellite was designated Object-D.

During the following month, Soviet Premier Nikita Khrushchev visited OKB-1 to see the R-7 missile. Korolev made the most of the opportunity. He displayed an Object-D mockup and described U.S. satellite plans. Khrushchev expressed concern that the satellite program might interfere with missile work, but he accepted Korolev's assurances to the contrary and endorsed the program.[14]

One of Korolev's selling points was that the R-7 ICBM was well along in development. It therefore stood a good chance of launching the first satellite because the United States had elected to build an entirely new rocket for its satellite effort. The Soviet engineer's assessment was not far off the mark.

On August 3, 1955, the Stewart Committee had approved the Project Vanguard plan of the Naval Research Laboratory (NRL) for an IGY science satellite. This committee was chaired by Homer Stewart of the Jet Propulsion Laboratory (JPL) at the California Institute of Technology, and it consisted of eight members appointed by the Department of Defense and the branch services. The committee chose Vanguard from a field of three rival projects: the Air Force's "World Series" plan, which envisioned launching a satellite weighing about 2,500 kilograms (about 5,000 pounds) on an Atlas missile with an upper stage; the Army's Project Orbiter, which proposed to launch a five-pound, poorly instrumented satellite on a Redstone missile with a Loki upper stage; and Vanguard, which had going for it an impressive suite of science instruments but which required the development of a new rocket based partly on the Viking sounding rocket. The Air Force plan was eliminated because it might interfere with missile development. The Stewart Committee had difficulty choosing between the Army and NRL plans. The Army booster clearly won out over the Vanguard rocket, which existed only on paper, while the NRL satellite's impressive instrument complement was in keeping with the scientific spirit of the IGY. For a time, the committee considered launching the NRL satellite on the Army booster, but its members worried that interservice rivalry might delay the satellite past the IGY.[15] By some accounts, the final vote could have gone for either Orbiter or Vanguard, and it may in fact have been decided in the end by the absence of one member because of illness.[16]

The Vanguard program was officially started on September 9, 1955, with a plan to build six vehicles. Of these, one was expected to reach orbit. The program had a budget of $20 million and an eighteen-month timetable leading to first orbital launch. The Object-D program began officially on February 25, 1956, with satellite assembly beginning on March 5 and launch targeted for the spring of 1957.[17] Both the U.S. and Soviet programs immediately fell behind schedule.

On September 14, 1956, Korolev addressed the Presidium of the Soviet Academy of Sciences to plead for additional support in meeting the target launch date. He complained that subcontractors were not making required deliveries. Korolev had become anxious when he received a report—mistaken, as it turned out—that a September 1956 missile test at Cape Canaveral had been a failed satellite launch attempt.

Sergei P. Korolev (1906–1966), Russian rocket and spacecraft pioneer.

In addition, the R-7 engine modified for satellite launches was not performing at the thrust level expected. Korolev drove himself and his staff mercilessly to solve the problem, but he finally had to change his plans. On January 5, 1957, he formally proposed reducing the weight of the first Soviet satellite to improve its chances of being first in space. He cited the supposed failed U.S. satellite launch and his belief that the United States could try again in early 1957. In fact, Korolev proposed two "simple satellites." PS-1 and PS-2, as they were known, would each weigh about 100 kilograms (220 pounds). The Soviet Council of Ministers approved the change on February 15, 1957.[18]

Korolev did not need to drive himself and his staff so hard, for in the United States, Vanguard also had problems. Between September 1955 and April 1957, the program's cost shot up from $20 million to $110 million. On May 3, 1957, the Bureau of the Budget sent an urgent memorandum on the overruns to President Eisenhower. He placed the issue on the agenda of the May 10 NSC meeting.

John Hagen, Vanguard's program director, and Detlov Bronk, president of the National Academy of Sciences, may have felt buoyed by the successful second Vanguard test launch on May 1. TV-1, as it was known, tested a rocket consisting of a liquid-fueled Vanguard first stage (a modified Viking sounding rocket) and a prototype solid-fueled Vanguard third stage. Hagen attempted to justify the program on the basis of its expected scientific return, and Bronk appealed to Eisenhower's vision of the future, declaring that the first satellite launch would mark the start of a new historical epoch. The President, however, would have none of that—he kept the discussion focused on Vanguard's escalating cost. Eisenhower complained that the scientists had "gold-plated" their instruments and produced plans for satellites larger and more elaborate than those he had approved. The act of launching the satellite was what would create prestige, not the instruments it carried, he said. ("Freedom of space" was not directly mentioned, although the NSC 5520 directive was.) Eisenhower grudgingly admitted that the United States had little choice but to continue the costly program because it had publicly announced that it would launch a satellite. He insisted, however, that the total cost be held to $110 million. He stated that, while six Vanguards were being built, there was no reason to suppose that all six would be launched. The Vanguard program might end as soon as it succeeded in placing a satellite in orbit. There was little hint of urgency.[19]

The IGY began on July 1, 1957, and a few days later, on July 5, the Central Intelligence Agency (CIA) reported to Deputy Secretary of Defense Donald Quarles that a Soviet satellite launch might occur as early as the birthday anniversary of Russian rocket pioneer Konstantin Tsiolkovskiy on September 17. This intelligence apparently excited little interest among members of the Eisenhower administration who learned of it.[20] Korolev might have been gratified at the time to know that the CIA supposed that he might launch a satellite as early as September, for his R-7 rocket was having trouble. By the end of July, it failed three times in succession. Finally, on August 21, 1957, the missile flew successfully for the first time. The flight was announced to the world on August 27, but many in the United States were skeptical that the Soviets had accomplished the world's first ICBM test. A second, less publicized test on September 7 was also successful.

The September 17 target date had to slip, however. On September 20, the State Commission for the PS-1 satellite authorized an October 6 launch from Baikonur Cosmodrome in Soviet Kazakhstan. Fearful that the United States might launch its satellite during the September 30–October 5 IGY Rockets and Satellites Conference in Washington, Korolev advanced PS-1's launch to October 4.[21] The R-7 rocket modified for launching PS-1 was placed on the pad on October 3. Fueling began at

The announcement by the Soviets of the intention to launch an Earth satellite during the IGY. This photo was taken at the Legation of the Soviet Union in Copenhagen, Denmark, during the 6th International Astronautical Congress, August 1955, shortly after the Americans announced their intentions to launch a satellite. Left to right: Mr. Vereschetin and Mr. Sannikov of Soviet State Security; Kyrill F. Ogorodikov, professor of astronomy, Leningrad University; and Leonid Ivanovich Sedov, specialist in mechanics, Soviet Academy of Sciences.

5:45 a.m., Baikonur time, the next day, and the rocket lifted off sixteen hours later. Six minutes after liftoff, PS-1—soon renamed Sputnik—ejected from its expended carrier rocket to became a second moon of Earth. A new age of exploration was under way.

One Small Ball in the Air: October 4, 1957–November 3, 1957

On Friday, October 4, 1957, U.S. domestic news was dominated by Eisenhower's decision to send troops to Little Rock, Arkansas, to enforce civil rights legislation integrating the schools. When Americans heard about Sputnik, some stepped outside to look for the racing spot of light moving across the crisp autumn sky. Others stayed inside to watch the premiere of a comedy television program called *Leave it to Beaver*.

The Eisenhower administration viewed the Soviet satellite less as a military threat than as a boost to its behind-the-scenes efforts to establish the principle of "freedom of space" ahead of eventual military reconnaissance satellite launches. Sputnik overflew international boundaries, yet it aroused no diplomatic protests. Four days after Sputnik's launch, on October 8, Donald Quarles summed up a discussion he had with Eisenhower: "the Russians have . . . done us a good turn, unintentionally, in establishing the concept of freedom of international space. . . . The President then looked ahead . . . and asked about a reconnaissance [satellite] vehicle."[22]

That same day, in response to mounting public alarm, U.S. Secretary of State John Foster Dulles sent White House Press Secretary James Hagerty a memorandum on the Soviet satellite. Dulles called the Sputnik launch "an event of considerable technical and scientific importance," but he hastened to add that its "importance should not be exaggerated . . . the value of the satellite to mankind will for a long time be highly problematical." Furthermore, the Dulles asserted, "the United States . . . has not neglected this field. It already has a capability to utilize outer space for missiles and it is expected to launch an earth satellite during the present geophysical year in accordance with a program that has been under orderly development over the past two years."[23]

The furor over Sputnik's launch took several days to build as opinion-makers struggled to interpret the event in the wider context of U.S. national security. Dulles's comments became the basis for the Eisenhower administration's response to the Soviet satellite. The day after Hagerty received the memorandum, on October 9, 1957, Eisenhower faced the press for the first time since the launch. Seeking to calm Congress and the public, he assured reporters that Sputnik contained "no additional threat to the United States," adding that "from what [the Soviets] say, they have put one small ball in the air." When asked how his administration could have let the Soviets be first in space, Eisenhower said that "no one ever suggested to me . . . a race except, of course, more than once we would say, well, there is going to be a great psychological advantage in world politics to putting the thing up, but . . . in view of the real scientific character of our development, there didn't seem to be a reason for just trying to grow hysterical about it." He added that he had provided the U.S. satellite and missile efforts with funds "to the limit of my ability . . . and that is all I can do."[24]

Eisenhower's greatest error in the Sputnik "crisis" was his failure to appreciate the psychological dimension of launching the first satellite. Far from being about science solely, Sputnik came to be about the way Americans saw themselves. Many saw Sputnik as

Before a national television audience, President Dwight D. Eisenhower displays a nose cone from a Jupiter-C missile on August 7, 1957.

confirmation that the Soviets had an operational ICBM, a feat the United States, supposedly the technological leader of the world, could not yet match.[25] The administration's efforts to quell fears immediately backfired. Many interpreted Eisenhower's statements as evidence that he was out of touch. NASA Historian Roger Launius has summed up the (unfair) popular appraisal of Eisenhower at the time: "A smiling incompetent . . . a 'do-nothing,' golf-playing president mismanaging events. . . ."[26] His comments looked weak placed beside the alarmist statements emanating from Congress. Typical of these were comments by Democratic Senator Richard Russell of Georgia, chair of the Armed Services Committee: "We now know beyond a doubt that the Russians have the ultimate weapon—a long-range missile capable of delivering atomic and hydrogen explosives across continents and oceans. . . ."[27]

Many criticized Eisenhower for pinching pennies and making ill-informed decisions without free debate at the expense of national technological leadership and security. As *Aviation Week* Editor-in-Chief Robert Hotz stated in the first of a series of scathing post-Sputnik editorials:

> We believe that the people of this country have a right to know the facts about the relative positions of the U.S. and the Soviet Union in this technological race which is perhaps the most significant event of our times. They have the right to find out why a nation with our vastly superior scientific, economic, and military potential is being at the very least equaled and perhaps surpassed by a country that less than two decades ago couldn't even play in the same scientific ball park. They also have the right to make decisions as to whether they want their government to maintain our current leadership of the free world regardless of the cost in dollars and sweat. . . . They are not decisions to be made arbitrarily by a clique of leaders in an ivory tower or on a golf course.[28]

On the day Eisenhower faced the media, Senate Majority Leader Lyndon Johnson received his first post-Sputnik briefing from the Pentagon. Johnson was entertaining friends at his ranch near Austin, Texas, when the Sputnik news broke. "In the Open West you learn to live closely with the sky," he wrote later of the night of October 4. "It is part of your life. But now, somehow, in some new way, the sky seemed almost alien."[29] In addition to an alien sky over the Texas hill country, Johnson saw in Sputnik an issue important to the nation that could advance his career and party. According to Johnson aide Glen Wilson, Johnson launched plans that very night for a public investigation into the state of U.S. satellite and missile programs in the Senate Preparedness Subcommittee, which he chaired.[30]

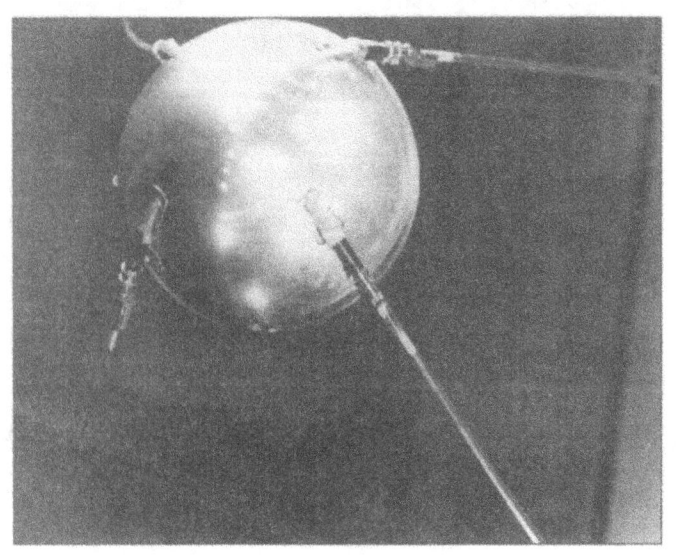

The Sputnik I spacecraft.

Eisenhower publicly downplayed concerns over Sputnik, but behind the scenes, he took modest steps to counter the Soviet propaganda victory. On October 8, he had asked outgoing Secretary of Defense Charles Wilson to order the Army Ballistic Missile Agency (ABMA) at Redstone Arsenal in Huntsville, Alabama, to ready a Jupiter-C rocket to launch a satellite. Not until November 8, however, did the command reach the Redstone Arsenal and become public.[31] The ABMA received authorization from the Army for two launch attempts. Project Vanguard transferred a science instrument—James Van Allen's radiation detector—from one of the later planned Vanguard satellites to the ABMA effort.

By then, the Eisenhower administration had twice as many reasons for launching a U.S. satellite as soon as possible. On November 3, 1957, Korolev's team had launched Sputnik II. The satellite, which included 508 kilograms (1,118 pounds) of payload, was a hastily prepared combination of the PS-2 satellite and a life support capsule for a dog, which was originally designed for brief sounding rocket flights. On board was a canine passenger named Laika.

The Birth of NASA: November 3, 1957– October 1, 1958

President Eisenhower spoke on television on November 7 as Sputnik I and Sputnik II orbited Earth. He displayed a missile nose cone recovered after a suborbital flight on a Jupiter-C rocket a few days before. Eisenhower's prepared statement focused on improving science and technology education, and he announced the appointment of Dr. James R. Killian, Jr., the president of the Massachusetts Institute of Technology, as his Special Assistant for Science and Technology. Killian's appointment was interpreted in Congress as a determination to put a civilian spin on the growing debate over the future course of U.S. space exploration.[32] Eisenhower confirmed this conviction during a November 13 speech on technical education in Oklahoma City, in which he spoke publicly of a civilian space agency for the first time.

On Monday, November 25, the Senate Preparedness Subcommittee hearings commenced. These hearings kept Lyndon Johnson and the missile and space issues in the public eye for several weeks. Seventy-three witnesses provided their assessments of the state of U.S. missile technology and interpretations of the events leading up to Sputnik. John Hagen told Johnson that Project Vanguard could have beat Sputnik I into orbit if it had been afforded a higher priority.[33] He reported that he had asked for higher priority in 1955 but never received a response.[34]

Donald Quarles testified that, in retrospect, the job of launching an IGY satellite should have been given to the Army in 1955. He hastened to add, however, that "[t]aking the missile program as a whole and comparing their [the Soviet] program with our own, I estimate that as of today our program is ahead." He told subcommittee chair Johnson that the United States was ahead in electronics, but it was hard to say which country was ahead in missiles. It was true, he said, that the Russians had a more powerful rocket engine, but "one would be even there cautious about the statement that they were ahead of us in rocket engines." He reported that since Sputnik I, there had been no acceleration of U.S. rocket programs—none was necessary. Johnson interpreted this as complacency on the part of the Pentagon and the Eisenhower White House. "The net of it is," he drawled, "that the American people can have adequate defense and eat their cake too—and even have whipped cream on it."[35]

The subcommittee did not explore specifically how the United States should organize to explore space, but this complex and contentious issue was a subtext. As the hearings continued into early December, the Eisenhower administration transferred to the White House the Science Advisory Committee of the Defense Department's Office of Defense Mobilization. It became the nucleus of the new President's Science Advisory Committee (PSAC), which was constituted in part to consider how best to organize the U.S. space effort. Five new members were added, including James Doolittle, chair of the National Advisory Committee on Aeronautics (NACA), which was created in 1916 to be the civilian government organization performing research into aviation.

An exploded view of the Sputnik I spacecraft.

Explorer I sits on the launch pad venting before launch, January 31, 1958. (NASA photo 97-H-482)

The push to organize a national space program received new impetus on December 6, when the Vanguard TV-3 rocket climbed about a yard above its Florida launch pad before falling back and exploding. The mission was to have been the first all-up test of the new Vanguard rocket. TV-3 carried a one-and-seven-tenths-kilogram (three-and-a-quarter-pound) test satellite derided by Soviet leader Khrushchev as an "orange."[36]

On December 30, James Killian wrote a memorandum to Eisenhower in which he noted that many scientists held "deeply felt convictions" opposing Defense Department control of the space program because they felt it would limit space research strictly to military objectives and would tar all U.S. space activity as military in nature. He then offered some organizational alternatives for space that he believed would provide "the means for non-military basic space research while at the same time taking advantage of the immense resources of the military missile and recon satellite programs." Killian proposed a Defense Department–operated "central space laboratory with a very broad charter," which he likened to the Los Alamos National Laboratory. He wrote that the administration might also "encourage NACA to extend its space research and provide it with the necessary funds to do so."[37, 38]

The ABMA's Explorer satellite program continued in its backup role following the Vanguard TV-3's failure in December. Range restrictions prevented simultaneous Vanguard and Explorer launch preparations. The ABMA's opportunity arrived on January 26 when the backup to the ill-fated TV-3 vehicle, the Vanguard TV-3BU, had to "stand down" pending a second stage engine replacement. This gave the Huntsville team until about February 1 to make a launch attempt. The first attempt on January 30 was scrubbed because of unfavorable winds. The jet stream shifted north the next day, however. At 10:48 p.m. Eastern time on January 31, 1958, Explorer I lifted off on top of a Jupiter-C. At 12:51 a.m. on February 1, a successful orbit was confirmed.

Explorer I's success encouraged supporters of a crash effort to recoup lost U.S. prestige by launching an automated probe to the Moon. The proposal, first discussed in Barcelona the morning after Sputnik, came up for discussion in the February 4, 1958, Legislative Leadership Meeting at the White House—an opportunity for Republican congressional leaders and the Eisenhower administration to compare notes.

Interestingly, despite his problems with the Sputniks, Eisenhower remained cold to reaping the prestige benefits of a Moon shot. The meeting minutes state that Eisenhower was "firmly of the opinion that the rule of reason had to be applied to these Space projects—that we couldn't pour unlimited funds into these costly projects where there was nothing of early value to the Nation's security. . . . [I]n the present situation, the President mused, he would rather have a good Redstone than be able to hit the moon, for we didn't have any enemies on the moon!" When Senator William Knowland pointed out the prestige value of being first to hit the Moon, Eisenhower relented partly, saying that if a rocket now available could do the job, work should go ahead. The President stressed, however, that he "didn't want to rush into an all-out effort on each of these possible glamor performances without a full appreciation of their great cost."[39]

Meanwhile, Congress discussed alternatives for organizing the U.S. space program. House Majority Leader John McCormack, a Massachusetts Democrat, called for a presidentially appointed

National Science Council, while another faction sought to put the space program under control of the Atomic Energy Commission (AEC). Democratic Senators John McClellan of Arkansas and Hubert Humphrey of Minnesota called for the establishment of a Department of Science and Technology headed by a Cabinet-level secretary, a proposal Eisenhower opposed.[40]

Although making the NACA the nucleus of a civilian space program did not at first find supporters in Congress, it soon became the favorite option of the PSAC. On February 4, the Purcell Panel was established to consider organizational alternatives for space. The panel was named for Nobel Laureate Edward Purcell, who was appointed to the PSAC in December when it transferred to the White House. On February 21, S. Paul Johnston, director of the Institute for Aeronautical Sciences and a participant in the panel, summed up the issue of space program organization as one of "exploration" versus "control." The latter, he said, was a military function. He cited four possible organizational alternatives:

- *Establish a new government agency.* This would, he wrote, take too much time.

- *Assign the space program to the AEC.* In political terms, this proposal was well supported in Congress, but the AEC had no experience in the space field, and its new responsibilities would constitute a distraction from its vital atomic energy roles. Johnston dubbed the alternative "the least practical."

- *Establish the NACA as the controlling agency.* Johnston pointed out that "[e]xtending [the NACA's] interests into space technology would seem to be a logical evolutionary step from its research activities of the past 40-odd years."

- *Assign space to the Advanced Research Projects Agency (ARPA) of the Defense Department.* ARPA was created on February 7, 1958. "ARPA could take on the job with a minimum of additional legislation," wrote Johnston, "but military interests might outweigh the purely scientific and civil aspects. . . . It would be difficult to avoid security restrictions, and participation in international programs of a purely scientific nature might thereby be hampered."[41]

On February 6, the Senate formed an ad hoc Special Committee on Space and Astronautics chaired by Lyndon Johnson. On March 5, the same day Vanguard 1 reached orbit, the House of Representatives established the ad hoc Select Committee on Astronautics and Space Exploration with House Majority Leader John McCormack as chair. Also on March 5, the President's Advisory Committee on Government Organization chair Nelson Rockefeller, James Killian, and Bureau of the Budget Director Percival Brundage recommended to Eisenhower that "leadership of the civil space effort be lodged in a strengthened and redesignated National Advisory Committee for Astronautics."[42] Eisenhower immediately authorized their proposal and assigned the Bureau of the Budget to draft the required legislation.

Dr. William H. Pickering, Dr. James A. Van Allen, and Dr. Wernher von Braun (left to right) hoist a model of Explorer I and the final stage after the successful launching on January 31, 1958. (NASA photo 78-H-136)

The first test launch of the Vanguard launch vehicle for the U.S.-IGY Earth Satellites Program to place a satellite in Earth orbit to determine atmospheric density and conduct geodetic measurements. A malfunction in the first stage caused the vehicle to lose thrust after two seconds, and the vehicle was destroyed.

In a speech to a joint session of Congress on April 2, Eisenhower called for a NACA-based civilian National Aeronautics and Space Agency (NASA). He also handed down a directive ordering the NACA and the Defense Department to begin arranging the transfer of nonmilitary Department of Defense space assets to the NACA. On April 14, Lyndon Johnson and New Hampshire Republican Styles Bridges introduced the Senate version of the NASA bill (S-3609), and John McCormack introduced the House version (HR-11881). Hearings commenced the following day.

On May 1, James Van Allen announced that radiation detectors aboard Explorer I and Explorer III (launched March 26) had been swamped by high radiation levels at certain points in their orbits. This pointed to the existence of powerful radiation belts surrounding Earth. The detection of the Van Allen Belts was the first major space discovery. Supporters of Eisenhower's methodical approach to space exploration capitalized on the find, pointing out that the Soviet Union's two heavy Sputniks had accomplished no equivalent scientific feat. In fact, the Soviets had not launched a new satellite since Sputnik II in November.

On May 5, NACA chair James A. Doolittle testified to the House Committee on Astronautics and Space Exploration that the U.S. civilian space program had "two focused objectives—gaining scientific data using automated probes and sending into space craft that will carry men on voyages of exploration." Branding an early Moon shot a "stunt," Doolittle added that "[i]n our programming we should keep our eyes focused on these objectives. The fact that the Russians may accomplish some specific objectives in their space programs first should not in itself be permitted to divert us from our own designated objectives."[43]

Korolev's team had not stopped work since Sputnik II. On May 15, Korolev finally launched the conical, 1,330-kilogram (2,926-pound) Object-D satellite. Academician Sedov declared, "The new Sputnik . . . could easily carry a man with a stock of food and supplementary equipment."[44] The sheer size of the satellite triggered new recriminations and new calls for action. *Aviation Week* editor-in-chief Robert Hotz again articulated well the mood in the U.S. space community:

> Successful launching of the 3000-lb Soviet Sputnik III should dispel most of the wishful thinking that has hung over the U.S. space policy since the fiery plunge of Sputnik II into the Caribbean [on April 14]. It proves once again that the Soviets' early Sputniks were no lucky accidents. It proves that the Soviet space program is a well-organized, consistent effort that is attempting to progress in significant increments rather than simply shooting for some spectacular, international propaganda stunt. It also indicates that the Soviet program has solid and consistent support not subject to the ups and downs of top level policy changes or political whims of the moment. . . . We are still debating in Congress the advisability of establishing a National Aeronautics and Space Agency. We hope Sputnik III will shake some of the Congressional nitpickers out of their lofty perches and prod them into action on this vital measure.[45]

Hotz soon got his wish. The House NASA bill passed on June 2, with the Senate version following on June 16. The most important conflict between the bills was the structure and composition of a committee advising the agency's director. The House bill—which Eisenhower favored—made provision for a relatively weak seventeen-member advisory committee, while the Senate bill had a strong seven-member policy board. A bipartisan nineteen-member blue ribbon panel chaired by Johnson produced a joint version that retained the strong policy board. President Eisenhower continued his opposition to the policy board on the grounds that it would usurp presidential authority. Eisenhower and Johnson met at the White House on July 7 to break the impasse. Johnson suggested that the president serve as chair of the policy board, and Eisenhower agreed.[46] The blue ribbon panel met for the final time on July 15, changing the policy board's name to the National Aeronautics and Space Council. Congress passed the final version of the bill on July 16, and President Eisenhower signed it into law on July 29, 1958.

The National Aeronautics and Space Act of 1958 (Public Law 85–568) stated that the NACA would become NASA after ninety days unless the transition was proclaimed sooner by the NASA administrator. On August 8, Eisenhower nominated T. Keith Glennan, the president of the Case Institute of Technology in Cleveland, Ohio, to be NASA's first administrator. He nominated NACA Director Hugh Dryden as deputy administrator. The Senate confirmed the nominations with little debate on August 14. On August 19, the Department of Defense and NASA agreed to transfer nonmilitary space projects, but they deferred the actual transfers until after NASA was in place. Glennan and Dryden were sworn in on August 20.

On August 17, the United States attempted its first Moon shot, an ARPA lunar orbiter on a Thor missile with an Able-1 upper stage. The Air Force Thor first stage exploded after seventy-seven seconds, destroying the thirty-eight-kilogram (eighty-four-pound) probe.

On September 4, Eisenhower appointed his fellow National Aeronautics and Space Council members. These included Glennan, Detlov Bronk, and James Doolittle. Glennan proclaimed NASA ready to succeed the NACA on September 25.

On October 1, 1958, NASA officially opened for business with five facilities inherited from the NACA: Lewis Research Center in Ohio, Langley Research Center and the Wallops rocket test range in Virginia, and Ames Research Center and the Muroc aircraft test range in California. That same day, Eisenhower issued an executive order transferring space projects and appropriations from other space programs to NASA. These gave NASA 8,240 staff (8,000 from the NACA) and a budget of approximately $340 million.

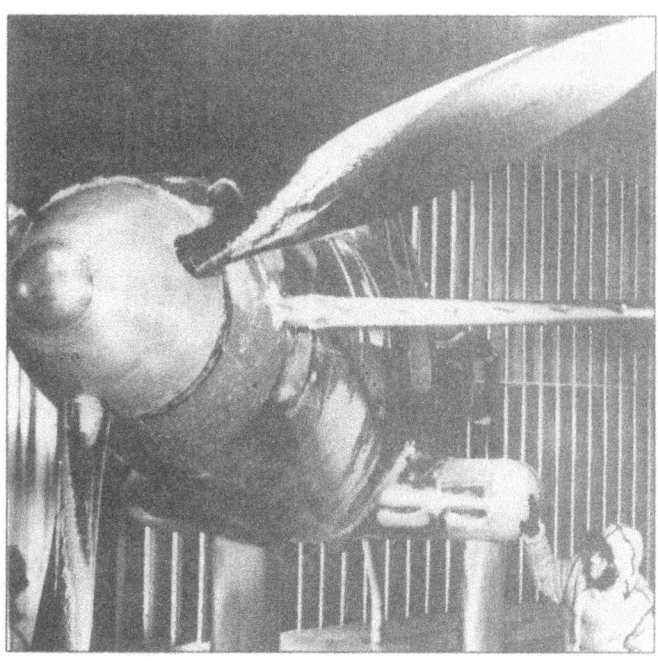

Icing research is under way during the 1940s at the Lewis Research Center in Cleveland, Ohio, one of the NACA's original facilities that became part of NASA.

This photo shows the original twelve-foot pressure wind tunnel at the Ames Research Center in Mountain View, California, shortly after its construction in 1946. Ames was another NACA facility that became part of NASA. (NASA photo 94-H-418)

Denouement—NASA's First Eighteen Months: October 1, 1958–December 20, 1960

On October 7, NASA formally organized its first "man-in-space" program, which was formally dubbed Project Mercury on November 26. ARPA's launch of the thirty-seven-and-a-half-kilogram (eighty-two-and-a-half-pound) Pioneer 1 on October 11 marked the resumption of U.S. efforts to reach the Moon. The probe failed to attain lunar orbit because of a problem in its second stage, but it did reach a record 115,000-kilometer (69,000-mile) apogee. Pioneer 1 burned up on October 13.

John Hagen transferred from NRL to NASA on November 5 to prepare for the Vanguard transfer, which duly moved to the agency on November 20 with $25 million in unexpended funds. Vanguard staff transferred from NRL on November 30. Personnel continued to work where they were located, however, with many making no physical transfer until the new Goddard Space Flight Center in Maryland opened in early 1960.

ARPA handed over Pioneer to NASA in November. The Army proved reluctant to carry out transfers and in fact fought them in public, through the press. On December 3, however, Eisenhower intervened, issuing an executive order that transferred JPL—then under Army jurisdiction—to NASA. The ABMA remained under Army control but agreed to make its resources responsive to NASA needs. In fact, NASA received authorization to bypass the Pentagon and deal directly with Huntsville.

On December 6, the almost six-kilogram (thirteen-pound) Pioneer 3 spacecraft carried out NASA's first foray beyond low-Earth orbit. The probe reached an apogee of 102,000 kilometers (61,200 miles) before falling back to Earth.

The IGY, the eighteen-month scientific program that spawned the space race and NASA, drew to a successful close on December 31. On January 2, 1959, Luna 1 (also known as Mechta, meaning "dream") perform the first lunar flyby. It soared past the Moon's ancient, battered craterscape at a distance of about 5,000 kilometers (3,000 miles). The just over 361-kilogram (795-pound) probe left Earth on an R-7 with an upper stage. Luna 1, intended to impact the lunar surface, instead became the first artificial object in solar orbit.

On March 3, NASA launched Pioneer 4. The little probe flew 60,000 kilometers (36,000 miles) past the Moon and entered solar orbit. Then, on April 9, NASA selected seven astronauts for the Mercury program.

The full-scale wind tunnel at the Langley Research Center in Hampton, Virginia. While Langley had a rich heritage in aeronautics work, engineers and scientists at Langley also became involved in space exploration with the birth of NASA. (NASA photo 90-H-190)

The Soviet Union succeeded in hitting the Moon on September 12, 1959, with the Luna 2 spacecraft, a near-twin of Luna 1. Luna 3 lifted off on the second anniversary of Sputnik I. The 278-kilogram (612-pound) flyby probe returned the first pictures of the Moon's far side on October 7.

The United States had lost another heat in the space race to the Soviet Union. This "second Sputnik" humiliation helped push the Moon closer to the center of U.S. space policy. On balance, though, the American response to Soviet Moon successes was less strident than those generated by the Sputniks. This time, the United States had a space agency in place to meet the challenge.

In early 1960, Korolev began launching a series of recoverable Korabl-Sputniks—test versions of the Vostok spacecraft that would launch the first humans into orbit in 1961. NASA, meanwhile, took delivery of its first Mercury capsule on April 1, 1960.

NASA's Origins and the Dawn of the Space Age

NASA Administrator T. Keith Glennan shows Associate Administrator Robert C. Seamans a model of the Mercury Redstone rocket on July 19, 1960.

President Lyndon B. Johnson addresses space workers at Cape Kennedy, Florida, on September 15, 1964. NASA Administrator James E. Webb is in the background. (NASA photo 64-H-2365)

The ABMA finally transferred to NASA on July 1, 1960, bringing with it its million-pound-thrust rocket engine and Saturn rocket programs. The ABMA formed the nucleus of the Marshall Space Flight Center. Later that month, on July 29, NASA issued a request for proposal for studies leading to the construction of the next generation of piloted spacecraft, called Apollo. The spacecraft was envisioned as an Earth-orbital vehicle with eventual circumlunar application.

In November 1960, John Kennedy defeated Eisenhower's Vice President, Richard Nixon, by a narrow margin, in part by emphasizing a "missile gap" that did not exist. On December 20, the President-elect announced his intention to make Vice President-elect Lyndon Johnson chair of the National Aeronautics and Space Council.

In the popular history of spaceflight, President Dwight Eisenhower is frequently relegated to the dark ages before the United States got moving and conquered the Moon. However, when Kennedy took charge in January 1961, the organizational apparatus and technology programs that made possible the spectacular events of NASA's first decade were already in place. Eisenhower had a legalistic agenda—establishing "freedom of space" as a principle of international law—and was fiscally conservative and loathe to be drawn into a battle of spectaculars with Khrushchev. A more dynamic leader might have been more emotionally satisfying at the time, but the four decades since the start of the space age demonstrate the firm foundations laid in the last half of the 1950s.

NOTES

1. Jay Holmes, *The Race for the Moon* (London: Victor Gollancz, 1962), pp. 46–47.

2. Constance McLaughlin Green and Milton Lomask, *Vanguard: A History* (Washington, DC: NASA SP-4202, 1970), p. 186.

3. Arthur C. Clarke, "Memoirs of an Armchair Astronaut (Retired)," in *Voices from the Sky* (New York: Pyramid, 1967), p. 153.

4. David Anderton, "Satellite's Glow Permeates Barcelona," *Aviation Week*, October 14, 1957, pp. 29–30.

5. Drawing on this new information, Asif A. Siddiqi has recently published a revealing account of events in the Soviet Union leading up to Sputnik's launch. See Asif A. Siddiqi, "Korolev, Sputnik, and the International Geophysical Year" (*http://www.hq.nasa.gov/office/pao/History/sputnik/siddiqi.html*). Similarly, R. Cargill Hall used recently declassified U.S. documents to trace the Eisenhower administration policy decisions that reined in the U.S. satellite program in the years immediately prior to Sputnik. See R. Cargill Hall, "Origins of U.S. Space Policy: Eisenhower, Open Skies, and Freedom of Space," in John M. Logsdon, gen. ed., with Linda J. Lear, Jannelle Warren-Findley, Ray A. Williamson, and Dwayne A. Day, *Exploring the Unknown: Selected Documents in the History of the U.S. Civil Space Program, Volume I: Organizing for Exploration* (Washington, DC: NASA SP-4407, 1995), pp. 213–29. Together, these articles paint a coherent picture of events in the United States and the Soviet Union leading up to the start of the space age.

6. Siddiqi, "Korolev, Sputnik, and the IGY."

7. Hall, "Origins of U.S. Space Policy," p. 217.

8. *Ibid.*, p. 220.

9. *Ibid.*, p. 221.

10. Siddiqi, "Korolev, Sputnik, and the IGY."

11. National Security Council, NSC 5520, "Draft Statement of Policy on U.S. Scientific Satellite Program," May 20, 1955, in Logsdon, gen. ed., *Exploring the Unknown*, 1: 308–13.

12. Siddiqi, "Korolev, Sputnik, and the IGY."

13. *Ibid.*

14. Asif Siddiqi, personal communication.

15. Holmes, *The Race for the Moon*, p. 51.

16. Green and Lomask, *Vanguard: A History*, p. 48.

17. Siddiqi, "Korolev, Sputnik, and the IGY."

18. *Ibid.*

19. "Memorandum of Discussion at the 322d Meeting of the National Security Council, Washington, D.C., May 10, 1957," in Logsdon, gen. ed., *Exploring the Unknown*, 1: 324–28.

20. Allen W. Dulles, Director of Central Intelligence, to The Honorable Donald Quarles, Deputy Secretary of Defense, July 5, 1957, in Logsdon, gen. ed., *Exploring the Unknown*, 1: 329–30.

21. Siddiqi, "Korolev, Sputnik, and the IGY."

22. Walter A. McDougall, . . . *The Heavens and the Earth: A Political History of the Space Age* (New York: Basic Books, 1985), p. 134.

23. John Foster Dulles to James C. Hagerty, October 8, 1957, in Logsdon, gen. ed., *Exploring the Unknown*, 1: 331.

24. "Impact of Russian Satellite to Boost U.S. Research Effort," *Aviation Week*, October 14, 1957, pp. 28–29.

25. This was not in fact correct. Only four R-7s were ever deployed as ICBMs, and these were quickly withdrawn from service as too difficult to prepare for launch and extremely vulnerable to attack. The R-7 instead became the most-used Soviet space launcher, and it is still in service today, with more than 1,200 launches to its credit.

26. Roger D. Launius, "Sputnik and the Origins of the Space Age" (*http://www.hq.nasa.gov/office/pao/History/sputnik/sputorig.html*).

27. Katherine Johnsen, "Senate Group Probes Satellite Progress," *Aviation Week*, October 14, 1957, pp. 31–32.

28. Robert Hotz, "Sputnik in the Sky," *Aviation Week*, October 14, 1957, p. 21.

29. Launius, "Sputnik and the Origins of the Space Age."

30. Glen P. Wilson, "How the Space Act Came to Be," unpublished manuscript in NASA Historical Reference Collection, NASA Headquarters, Washington, DC, p. 1.

31. Green and Lomask, *Vanguard: A History*, p. 202.

32. Wilson, "How the Space Act Came to Be," p. 4.

33. Green and Lomask, *Vanguard: A History*, p. 204.

34. "Democratic Leaders Attack Administration Sputnik Reaction," *Aviation Week*, December 9, 1957, pp. 31–32.

35. *Ibid.*

36. "Four Objects Reported in Sputnik Orbit," *Aviation Week*, May 26, 1958, pp. 28–29.

37. J.R. Killian, Jr., "Memorandum on Organizational Alternatives for Space Research and Development," December 30, 1957, in Logsdon, gen. ed., *Exploring the Unknown*, 1: 628–631.

38. Before Killian's memorandum became public, some attributed the suggestion that the NACA form the basis of the space program to Orval Cooke, the president of the Aircraft Industries Association. In early January 1958, Cooke told a meeting of the Institute of Aeronautical Sciences that key decisions, not new agencies, were the way to a vigorous U.S. space program. He proposed that the NACA be made the U.S. national space agency. The NACA, he said, "has been conducting research and studies in scientific fields leading to man's conquest of space for more than a decade." See "Key to Space," *Aviation Week*, January 20, 1958, p. 25. At about the same time, the NACA began to promote itself as part of an interagency space program, including the Defense Department, the National Science Foundation, and the National Academy of Sciences. See Robert Rosholt, *An Administrative History of NASA: 1958–1963* (Washington, DC: NASA SP-4101, 1966), p. 8.

39. L.A. Minnich, Jr., "Legislative Leadership Meeting, Supplementary Notes," February 4, 1958, in Logsdon, gen. ed., *Exploring the Unknown*, 1: 631–32.

40. "Congress Draws Battle Lines for Outer-Space Control," *Aviation Week*, February 3, 1958, p. 37

41. S. Paul Johnston, "Memorandum for Dr. J. R. Killian, Jr., Preliminary Observations on the Organization for the Exploitation of Outer Space," February 21, 1958, in Logsdon, gen. ed., *Exploring the Unknown*, 1: 632–36.

42. President's Advisory Committee on Government Organization, Executive Office of the President, Memorandum for the President, "Organization for Civil Space Programs," March 5, 1958, p. 3.

43. Ford Eastman, "Doolittle Urges Adoption of Plan for Civil Control of Space Agency," *Aviation Week*, May 5, 1958, p. 32.

44. "Four Objects Reported in Sputnik Orbit," *Aviation Week*, May 26, 1958, pp. 28–29.

45. Robert Hotz, "Sputnik III and U.S. Space Policy," *Aviation Week*, May 26, 1958, p. 21.

46. Wilson, "How the Space Act Came to Be," p. 10.

Key Events

1954	*May 26*
Sergei Korolev submits a proposal to study launching a Soviet satellite.

October 4
The ruling body of the International Geophysical Year (IGY) calls for science satellite launches during the IGY.

1955	*February 14*
The Technological Capabilities Panel proposes launching a science satellite to establish the principle of "freedom of space."

March 14
The U.S. IGY Committee declares launching a science satellite during the IGY feasible.

May 27
President Eisenhower approves the U.S. IGY satellite plan.

July 29
White House Press Secretary James Hagerty announces the U.S. IGY satellite plan.

August 2
In Copenhagen, Academician Leonid Sedov announces that the Soviet Union will launch an IGY satellite.

August 3
The Stewart Committee selects Project Vanguard as the U.S. IGY satellite program.

August 30
Korolev receives approval to launch the Object-D satellite.

September 9
Project Vanguard begins officially.

1957	*July 1*
The IGY begins.

August 21
The R-7 intercontinental ballistic missile (ICBM) flies successfully for the first time.

October 4
Sputnik I is launched on a modified R-7 ICBM.

November 3
Sputnik II is launched carrying Laika.

November 8
The Department of Defense authorizes the U.S. Army Explorer as a backup to Project Vanguard.

November 13
Eisenhower makes his first public statement calling for a civilian space agency.

November 25
Lyndon Johnson opens hearings in the Senate Preparedness Subcommittee to review U.S. defense and space programs.

December 6
The Vanguard TV-3 launch fails.

1958 *January 31*
Explorer I is launched, becoming the first U.S. satellite.

April 2
President Eisenhower addresses Congress to propose the creation of a National Aeronautics and Space Administration (NASA), responsible for civilian space and aeronautical research.

May 1
James Van Allen announces the discovery of Earth's radiation belts.

May 15
Sputnik III is launched.

July 29
Eisenhower signs the National Aeronautics and Space Act of 1958 (Public Law 85–568), forming NASA, with the National Advisory Committee for Aeronautics (NACA) as its nucleus.

August 19
T. Keith Glennan is sworn in as NASA's first administrator; Hugh Dryden is deputy administrator.

October 1
NASA opens for business.

October 7
NASA formally organizes Project Mercury.

December 31
The IGY concludes.

1959 *January 2*
Luna 1 (Mechta, meaning "dream") is launched, becoming the first lunar flyby.

April 2
The Mercury 7 astronauts are selected.

September 12
Luna 2 is launched, resulting in the first lunar impact.

October 4
Luna 3 is launched, producing the first pictures of the Moon's far side.

1960 *July 1*
The George C. Marshall Space Flight Center is established with transfer of the Army Ballistic Missile Agency from the Army to NASA.

July 29
Project Apollo is announced.

December 20
President-elect John Kennedy announces that Vice President-elect Lyndon Johnson will chair the National Aeronautics and Space Council.

Document 1

Title: United States Information Agency, "World Opinion and the Soviet Satellite: A Preliminary Evaluation," October 17, 1957.

Source: White House Office of Special Assistant for National Security Affairs files, Eisenhower Library, Abilene, Kansas.

Less than two weeks after the launch of Sputnik I, the United States Information Agency conducted an informal analysis of public opinion on this subject. The analysis yielded four clear conclusions: (1) Soviet claims of scientific and technological superiority were widely accepted in the United States; (2) U.S. allies were concerned about a shift in the balance of military power; (3) the overall credibility of Soviet propaganda was greatly strengthened; and (4) American prestige was dealt a severe blow. The report also concluded that the near-hysteria in the United States in turn increased the level of concern in countries friendly to the United States.

CONFIDENTIAL / UNCLASSIFIED

OFFICE OF RESEARCH AND INTELLIGENCE

REPORT

WORLD OPINION AND THE SOVIET SATELLITE

A Preliminary Evaluation

October 17, 1957   P-94-57

THIS REPORT IS NOT A STATEMENT OF USIA POLICY

CONFIDENTIAL / UNCLASSIFIED

DECLASSIFIED
9 USIA ca. 5/18/93
Authority State Guidelines MSS-9
By DTH   NLE Date 11/26/93

WORLD OPINION AND THE SOVIET SATELLITE

A Preliminary Evaluation

One week after the USSR announced that it had launched an earth satellite, a number of broad major effects on world public opinion appeared clear:

1. Soviet claims of scientific and technological superiority over the West and especially the U.S. have won greatly widened acceptance.

2. Public opinion in friendly countries shows decided concern over the possibility that the balance of military power has shifted or may soon shift in favor of the USSR.

3. The general credibility of Soviet propaganda has been greatly enhanced.

4. American prestige is viewed as having sustained a severe blow, and the American reaction, so sharply marked by concern, discomfiture and intense interest, has itself increased the disquiet of friendly countries and increased the impact of the satellite.

A few instances of immediate reactions illustrate significantly the promptness, diversity and scope of the impact reported. Mexican editors expressed diminished interest in USIS scientific feature articles, and frankly said that they were looking to Soviet sources for such material. In Tehran, officials of the Iranian Government considered the satellite such a blow to U.S. prestige that they displayed uneasy embarrassment in discussing it with Americans. Representatives of the Western European Union Assembly meeting in Strasbourg severely criticized the U.S. for falling behind in the arms race. In Japan, members of the Liberal Democratic Party agitated against further increases in conventional military forces.

The satellite is, of course, most readily accepted as proof of scientific and technical leadership by those with the least scientific and political sophistication. The degree to which informed scientific

- 2 -

and political opinion believes that the USSR has surpassed the U.S. in scientific capability cannot yet be assessed. Sophisticated opinion is, of course, far less likely to be impressed merely by the drama of the satellite or its being a "first." It will be much slower to form its opinion of the fundamental implications of the Soviet achievement as an index of the level of Soviet science, and of the relative capabilities of the U.S. and the USSR.

To this influential group, however, even temporary Soviet possession of a clear lead in missile research and technology underlines Soviet potential capacity to compete successfully in fields in which U.S. leadership has been generally taken for granted. The pattern may have changed from one in which the USSR was seen as seeking to catch up, to one in which the USSR and the US are viewed as in more or less level competition. This is clearly one of the aims of Soviet propaganda treatment, which can be expected to make a very strong effort to create and deepen the impression that the satellite marks a new era, and to make its launching a sort of Great Divide.

Although the informed intelligentsia may give only limited assent to Soviet assertions, this will not immediately or very greatly limit Soviet psychological gains. The technologically less advanced -- the audience most impressed and dazzled by the sputnik -- are often the audience most vulnerable to the attractions of the Soviet system. The crux of the long-range Soviet propaganda effort may be its ability to win acceptance for the validity of the Soviet system, especially among the newly independent or dependent peoples, largely preoccupied with establishing quickly the technological level that will assure economic viability and national progress. The satellite, presented as the achievement of the Soviet system, helps to lend credence to Soviet claims -- particularly if it is followed by comparable achievements unmatched by the West.

This audience does not merely include those most eager to find ways for rapid technological advancement. It is also the audience -- especially in its broadest mass and most illiterate depths -- most difficult to reach with cold fact and reasoned argument. It is, in fact, an audience difficult for the U.S. propagandist to reach at all with the resources at his disposal. The peculiar nature and dramatic appeal

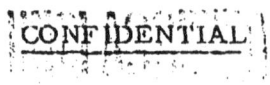

- 3 -

of the sputnik, making its passes over every region of the earth, are likely to give it peculiar impact among those least able to understand it. It will generate myth, legend and enduring superstition of a kind peculiarly difficult to eradicate or modify, which the USSR can exploit to its advantage, among backward, ignorant, and apolitical audiences particularly difficult to reach.

Assessment of the implications of the satellite -- following closely on the ICBM -- for the balance of military power probably follows the same general pattern. The distinction between military and scientific implications is often not being sharply drawn and appears hardly to be drawn at all among the least informed. The USSR is diligently seeking to create the impression that in this field too a watershed has been reached, and that a re-evaluation of relative military strength and positions must follow. Popular reaction will affect willingness to support conventional armaments, and also add support to Soviet claims that current Western positions on disarmament are outmoded.

The Soviet Union may well believe that it has succeeded in creating sufficient doubts about U.S. military superiority to give it decided advantages if it should choose to expand its psychological warfare by campaigns in either the classic "War of Nerves" or "Peace Campaign" pattern. It appears to be readying the psychological ground for such operations. To the extent that there is any substantial public conclusion that the USSR is leading in military power, the USSR appears to speak from strength not weakness. This psychological advantage could be exploited whether in seeking a detente or attempting an expansionist venture.

Soviet efforts to exploit the military significance of the scientific and technological victory it has registered are currently still largely indirect: they could, particularly if conducted with brusqueness, braggadocio, and bellicosity, become psychologically counterproductive, by underscoring the aggressive motives and methods of the Soviet system. They would, thus, raise in the very audiences they seek to impress doubts about the reality of Soviet desires for "peaceful coexistence" and about the likelihood that Soviet world dominance would further their national aspirations. It is too soon to judge whether Soviet awareness of this danger will continue

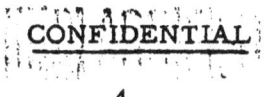

- 4 -

to impose effective restraints on their exploitation of recent or potential future propaganda successes.

Soviet awareness of the fact that maximum effective exploitation of their gains depends upon keeping a balance between "peacefulness" and "strength" in claiming achievements for the Soviet system, may tend to strengthen propaganda efforts designed to dramatize the willingness of the USSR to offer the peaceful fruits of these achievements to others, to extend "scientific and technical cooperation and assistance." They are, in fact, well launched on this competition in many areas.

To some extent, at this early stage, judgments are in suspension, particularly among the informed, and among those leaders whose attitudes are especially important to the U.S. interest. Much of this suspension of judgment stems, however, from confidence in the ability of the U.S. speedily to recapture lost ground and to surpass the USSR. Even if this expectation were considerably delayed in fulfilment, many of these persons would not modify their assessments of the relative desirability of the two systems. But this audience is not presumably a primary target of either U.S. or Soviet propaganda.

In judging the long-range significance of reaction, one finding of 1956 public opinion surveys in Western Europe and Japan is of particular interest. Asked whether they expected the U.S. or the USSR to emerge the stronger in peaceful "competitive coexistence" over the next twenty-five years, a substantial body of opinion answered "the USSR"; the average U.S. lead in the five chief West European countries was only eleven per cent.

A final point that deserves noting is the fact that the U.S. itself set the stage for assuring the impact of the sputnik — first by the fanfare of its own announcement of its satellite plans, second by creating the impression that we considered ourselves to have an invulnerable lead in this scientific and technological area, and third by the nature of the reaction within the U.S. All this has served to underscore the importance, implications, and presumed validity of Soviet performance and Soviet claims. American public anxiety, recrimination, and intense emotional interest have been widely noted abroad, and assiduously reported by Soviet media. The nature of U.S. public reaction in the immediate future will continue to be an important

- 5 -

factor in coloring the responses of other people. One moral that might be drawn is that a propagandist cannot have his crow and eat it too.

This has all helped to increase the credibility of Soviet propaganda, although presumably no U.S. reaction, however serene and poised, could have markedly diminished the basic gain in credibility derived from the incontestable fact that the Soviet system had achieved a difficult and impressive scientific "first". This gain in credibility, which can be exploited by almost every aspect of Soviet propaganda, may in the long run be the most durable and useful gain accruing to the USSR from the satellite.

In sum:

1. The Soviet satellite supplies an opportunity for the USSR to claim that it has opened a new era, marked by a spectacular overtaking of the U.S. in a vital field where we have been accustomed to count on superiority, and now competes with the U.S. as an equal.

2. Public opinion will, for a period that cannot now be forecast, be narrowly assessing the relative military positions of the U.S. and the USSR.

3. The USSR, in this same period, will have a clear advantage in the cold war, which it can exploit for either "peaceful" gestures or ventures in increased pressures -- or both simultaneously.

4. The satellite, presented as a demonstration that the Soviet system has gained scientific and technical superiority, lends increased appeal to that system, particularly in areas that view their problems as requiring the rapid achievement of a higher technological level.

5. General Soviet credibility has been sharply enhanced.

Document 2

Title: James R. Killian, Jr., "Memorandum on Organizational Alternatives for Space Research and Development," December 30, 1957.

Source: Dwight D. Eisenhower Papers, Eisenhower Library, Abilene, Kansas.

In the wake of Sputnik I and II, there was a wholesale reexamination of the U.S. organization for space-related activities. In 1955, when a scientific satellite program was initiated, it was given a low priority in comparison to other military efforts. At the time, there was concern that even a small civilian space program, if given too many resources, could adversely affect critical ballistic missile programs. The issue was not so much one of cost, but of the scarcity of human resources and development and test facilities. However, the political firestorm set off by the Soviet satellite brought into question the relatively low priority given the scientific space program. From the time the first Sputnik was launched until NASA was established, almost all elements of the government were engaged in the debate on how best to redress the situation and reestablish the prestige of the United States. The failure of the first Vanguard launch on December 6, 1957, only intensified the calls for change. Sputnik also created the necessary impetus in the White House for the creation of the position of presidential science advisor. On November 7, James R. Killian, the president of the Massachusetts Institute of Technology, was appointed to this position. One of Killian's first duties was to address the issue of alternatives for space research organization. Some of his thoughts in this early memorandum eventually formed the basis of the Eisenhower administration's future policy toward the creation of a space agency.

December 30, 1957

**MEMORANDUM ON ORGANIZATIONAL ALTERNATIVES
FOR SPACE RESEARCH AND DEVELOPMENT**

This memorandum is based upon the following assumptions:

A. That the Department of Defense proceeds with its announced plan for a Special Projects Division, reporting directly to the Secretary and including, as one of its major responsibilities, space research and development for the DOD.

B. That there is a broad area of non-military basic research relating to space which will command the interest and participation of scientists and engineers in a variety of non-government and government institutions.

With these assumptions in mind, we can proceed to a discussion of how the Government's sponsorship of space research and development can be handled and how the military and non-military programs can be related.

There have been proposals for a new Government agency analagous to either NACA or the AEC to handle all space research and development. In appraising this approach, the following considerations are of importance:

A. The DOD is committed to a space program and is in process of setting one up, although the nature of the program has not been clearly defined.

B. Those aspects of space research and development which relate to the use of missile engines, and the testing and launching of vehicles must be closely associated with DOD missile programs. The necessity of such close association may dictate the placing of responsibility in the DOD for the development, testing, and use of rocketry for putting up space vehicles. It would seem unwise for a new agency, independent of the DOD, to have to create and use test facilities other than those built by DOD.

It seems of greatest importance that the DOD's own space program be very closely related to its missile program or for the two programs at some time to be merged.

These considerations seem to indicate clearly that the DOD must play a major role in space research and development if we are to use the nation's manpower and facilities in this area to the greatest advantage.

The DOD will, of course, be primarily concerned with those aspects of space research and development which will have military value. It is hard at this stage, however, to separate out of space R&D those elements, however basic and purely scientific, which would not contribute to military objectives. It seems entirely feasible for DOD to be the major sponsor and entrepreneur of space research and development, both military and "non-military."

There are many scientists and others, however, who are opposed to the centralization of all space R&D under the DOD. There are deeply-felt convictions that the more purely scientific and non-military aspects of space research should not be under the control of the military. In the first place, such an arrangement might improperly limit the program to narrowly concerned military objectives. In the second place, it would tag our basic space research as military and place the U.S. in the unfortunate position before the world of apparently tailoring all space research to military ends.

The problem of planning our non-military space research, then, becomes one of devising the means for non-military basic space research while at the same time taking advantage of the immense resources of the military missile and recon satellite programs, there are several possible ways of doing this:

A. The D.O.D. as a part of its program would establish a central space laboratory with a very broad charter which would permit the conduct of the most basic sort of research as well as R and D, having obvious military objectives. We see the pattern for this is such a laboratory as the Los Alamos Scientific Laboratory of the A.E.C. Such a laboratory might also have the authority to sponsor research in civilian institutions.

B. The Department of Defense might confine itself to its military mission and some other agency or agencies external to the D.O.D. might engage in basic research. One obvious way of doing this would be to encourage N.A.C.A. to extend its space research and to provide it with the necessary funds to do so. A second method (and this one might be handled along with an N.A.C.A program) would be to provide funds either through the Department of Defense or otherwise to the National Research Council, the Council in turn sponsoring a series of projects in universities and industrial laboratories. The N.A.C.A. itself might do sub-contracting as indeed it does now to a limited extent. The problem here would be not to burden the N.A.C.A. with so large a program that the nature of N.A.C.A. would be changed. In its present form, it has been very successful but an undue enlargement of its program might reduce its effectiveness.

If either the N.A.C.A. or N.R.C. methods or both were followed it would be necessary to carefully to work out a cooperative arrangement with the D.O.D., for the D.O.D. would have to be an ative partner with these agencies.

Such combination of sponsorship and programs would probably be the most advantageous way of carrying on space research for meeting both military and non-military objectives.

In considering these various alternatives and means, it is important to keep in mind existing resources available in the D.O.D., the Army's ABMA has a highly competent group for space research. The Air Force's BMC has important resources, including a going program for the development of a recon satellite. Cal Tech's Jet Propulsion Laboratory has advantages and resources for space research - a laboratory which has been closely associated with the Army. In the interest of conserving man power and utilizing skill and experience already in being, these agencies must be considered in planning a new program. Someone or combination of these might well be made the nucleus of an extended program.

There should be some mechanism, however, which gives coherence to the broad program and which avoids a program encouraging inter-service rivalries.

The over-all plan must permit and provide for bold, imaginative research and planning. It must recognize the importance of providing the means and incentives for pure scientists to move effectively into space research without regard to practical applications. We must realize that in addition to such obvious objectives as space travel and reconnaissance there are extraordinary opportunities to extend our knowledge of the earth and its environment and enormously to extend astronomical observations. It may well be that these kinds of pure, non-practical research objectives may prove to be the most important and in the end the most practical.

The over-all plan, then, must keep steadily in view the need for those means and programs which will command the interest and participation of our best scientists. We must have far more than a program which appeals to the "space cadets." It must invoke, in the deepest sense, the attention of our best scientific minds if we as a nation are to become a leader in this field. If we do not achieve this, then other nations will continue to hold the leadership.

December 29, 1957   J. R. Killian, Jr.

Document 3

Title: L.A. Minnich, Jr., "Legislative Leadership Meeting, Supplementary Notes," February 4, 1958.

Source: Dwight D. Eisenhower Papers, Eisenhower Library, Abilene, Kansas.

The Soviets had orbited Sputnik I four months prior to the meeting recorded by Minnich. By this time, it was all but certain that a new space agency would be created; however, its responsibilities, form, and location were still undecided. The question of the military or civilian character of a new agency was discussed in a regularly scheduled meeting among President Eisenhower, Vice President Richard Nixon, other White House officials, and Republican leaders in Congress. The issue was raised in response to the impending reorganization of the Department of Defense, which was necessitated in part by the increasing sophistication and cost of weapons systems. Missiles and other space-related hardware were responsible for a significant portion of the technological revolution sweeping the military services at the time. At this time (February 1958), President Eisenhower had apparently not yet decided that most of the U.S. space program should be carried out under civilian auspices.

LEGISLATIVE LEADERSHIP MEETING

February 4, 1958

SUPPLEMENTARY NOTES

Postal Rates and Pay - In a long discussion of the situation concerning postal legislation, Sen. Carlson cautioned against trying to couple in one bill both the rate increase and pay raise. If that were done, he said, the opposition might write in a much larger pay increase than was proper, and that could be very embarrassing to the President. The President said he would not be embarrassed. On the contrary, he would be most concerned with what this Republican Party would look like.

P.L. 480 - Sen. Dirksen pointed out the interest of a number of farm-State Senators in having budgets other than Agriculture's charged with the costs of certain things done under the P.L. 480 program. Secretary Benson was very anxious to have this done, and cited figures (which Mr. Merriam, Bureau of the Budget) immediately questioned) pretending to show that only 10% of the P.L. 480 proceeds went to Agriculture. Much of it should be charged, he said, to the Mutual Security program. The President asked for a quick report of accurate statistics, and also pointed out to Sec. Benson that where we sold products below the market price, a loss occurred which is directly chargeable to Agriculture.

Outer Space Program - A question was raised as to whether a new Space Agency should be set up within Department of Defense (as provided in the pending Defense appropriation bill), or be set up as an independent agency. The President's feeling was essentially a desire to avoid duplication, and priority for the present would seem to rest with Defense because of paramountcy of defense aspects. However, the President thought that in regard to non-military aspects, Defense could be the operational agent, taking orders from some non-military scientific group. The National Science Foundation, for instance, should not be restricted in any way in its peaceful research.

Dr. Killian had some reservations as to the relative interest and activity of military vs. peaceful aspects, as did the Vice President who thought our posture before the world would be better if non-military research in outer space were carried forward by an agency entirely separate from the military.

There was some discussion of the prospect of a lunar probe. Dr. Killian thought this might be next on the list of Russian efforts. He had some doubt as to whether the United States should at this late date attempt to press a lunar probe, but the question would be fully canvassed by the Science Advisory Committee in the broad survey it had underway. Dr. Killian thought the U.S. might do a lunar probe in 1960, or perhaps get to it on a crash program by 1959. Sen. Saltonstall had heard, however, that it might even be accomplished in 1958, if pressed hard enough.

Legislative Supplementary Notes, February 4, 1958 - page 2

Dr. Killian outlined for the Leadership the various phases of future development (along the lines of the subsequent press release listing projects in the "soon", "later," and "much later" categories.)

Sen. Knowland complained about having to get his information about Space research from the Democratic Senator from Washington (Jackson) -- which was just as bad as having to learn from Mr. Symington anything there was to know about the Air Force.

The President was firmly of the opinion that a rule of reason had to be applied to these Space projects -- that we couldn't pour unlimited funds into these costly projects where there was nothing of early value to the Nation's security. He recalled the great effort he had made for the Atomic Peace Ship but Congress would not authorize it, even though in his opinion it would have been a very worthwhile project.

And in the present situation, the President mused, he would rather have a good Redstone than be able to hit the moon, for we didn't have any enemies on the moon!

Sen. Knowland pressed the question of hurrying along with a lunar probe, because of the psychological factor. He recalled the great impact of Sputnik, which seemed to negate the impact of our large mutual security program. If we are close enough to doing a probe, he said, we should press it. The President thought it might be OK to go ahead with it if it could be accomplished with some missile already developed or nearly ready, but he didn't want to just rush into an all-out effort on each one of these possible glamor performances without a full appreciation of their great cost. Also, there would have to be a clear determination of what agency would have the responsibility.

The Vice President reverted to the idea of setting up a separate agency for "peaceful" research projects, for the military would be deterred from things that had no military value in sight. The President thought Defense would inevitably be involved since it presently had all the hardware, and he did not want further duplication. He did not preclude having eventually a great Department of Space.

<u>Presidential Disability Legislation</u> - When Sen. Dirksen noted that a good many proposals were floating around the Senate, the President recalled that Mr. Rayburn had said that for his money there would never be a bill.

The President went on to say that he had been working with the Vice President on the matter. Of course, there would never be any reason for disagreement between them on this, but it seemed desirable to work it out in the best interests of the country -- on a personal basis. In addition, the President continued to want something on the statute book.

Mr. Rogers commented on one proposal on which he was consulted. It provided for an 8-man Commission, including the Vice President, Speaker, Majority and Minority Leaders. Mr. Rogers said he had had to comment

Legislative Supplementary Notes, February 4, 1958 - page 3

that this was clearly unconstitutional unless done as a Constitutional amendment. He didn't think it a desirable change since it would transfer power from the Executive to the Legislature.

L. A. Minnich, Jr.

Copy to:
  Mrs. Whitman (2)
  Mr. Minnich

Document 4

Title: S. Paul Johnston, Memorandum for Dr. J. R. Killian, Jr., "Activities," February 21, 1958, with attached: Memorandum for Dr. J. R. Killian, Jr., "Preliminary Observations on the Organization for the Exploitation of Outer Space," February 21, 1958.

Source: NASA Historical Reference Collection, NASA History Office, NASA Headquarters, Washington, D.C.

On February 4, 1958, President Eisenhower announced that science advisor James R. Killian had appointed a panel to recommend the outlines of a space program and the organization to manage it. The so-called "Purcell Panel" (General James H. Doolittle, NACA chair; Edwin Land, Polaroid Corporation president; Herbert York, Livermore Laboratory director; and Edward Purcell, Harvard University professor of physics), augmented by William Finan of the Bureau of the Budget and the staff support of S. Paul Johnston, who was director of the Institute for Aeronautical Sciences, assessed organizational alternatives for the proposed agency. The task of inventing an organization to manage a space program was a difficult one. The number and strength of the claimants for the right to direct the space program had peaked in the wake of Sputnik. Several bills were already pending before Congress that gave responsibility for space programs to the Department of Defense or to the Atomic Energy Commission. Johnston's thoughts on the subject eventually found their way into the March 5, 1958, memorandum to the president containing the formal proposal that the National Advisory Committee for Aeronautics (NACA) be reconstituted and given the responsibility for managing the nation's space program. In this copy of the memorandum, someone (possibly Killian) has made handwritten comments and changes to Johnston's text.

```
To  Unclassified
By authority of NAR=LTR 6/14/76
Changed by Marie          Date 6/23/76
```

THE WHITE HOUSE
WASHINGTON

February 21, 1958

MEMORANDUM FOR DR. J. R. KILLIAN, JR.

FROM: S. Paul JOHNSTON

SUBJECT: Activities

1. During the past week in accordance with your suggestion, I have conferred on the problem of organization and its legal implications with the following:

> James A. Perkins, Vice President, Carnegie Corporation
> John Cobb Cooper, Legal Consultant, Professor, International Air Law, McGill University
> Dr. James Fisk, Vice President, Bell Telephone Laboratories
> John J. Corson, McKinsey & Company
> Don K. Price, Vice President, Ford Foundation
> Dr. Edward Mason, Harvard University
> Dean David Cavers, Harvard Law

The above are in addition to the people we have talked to in the Bureau of the Budget at the meeting which you attended on Monday.

2. As a result of the above conferences I have prepared the attached memorandum which summarizes the various views which have been expressed on the organizational problem and which makes a recommendation which is my own but which appears to be consistent with the discussions of the past week. To date this has been discussed only with Dr. James Fisk.

S. P. Johnston

Attachment

THE WHITE HOUSE
WASHINGTON

February 21, 1958

MEMORANDUM FOR DR. J. R. KILLIAN, JR.

PRELIMINARY OBSERVATIONS ON THE ORGANIZATION FOR THE
EXPLOITATION OF OUTER SPACE

The exploitation of any unknown areas involves two distinct objectives, - one, <u>exploration</u> and two, <u>control</u>. The first is largely a scientific operation and the second largely military.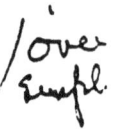

At the present time plans for the exploitation of outer space fall more nearly into civilian-scientific areas rather than into military areas. The "take" from the probing of outer space by rockets, satellites and interplanetary vehicles will be of more direct interest to the scientist than to the strategist. We can discount at this point most of the "Buck Rogers" type of thinking which anticipates hordes of little men in space helmets firing disintegrators into each other from flying saucers. Certainly, ICBM's will transit portions of outer space in performing their missions, but for the moment the chief military interest lies in better methods of surveillance, communications and long-range weather forecasting.

The potential space explorations in the immediate future are well outlined in a paper dated 14 February 1957 titled "Basic Objectives of a Continuing Program of Scientific Research in Outer Space" by Hugh Odishaw, Executive Director of the U.S. National Committee for the IGY of the National Academy of Sciences. A good layman's summary of the same subject appeared in a recent issue of LIFE magazine by Dr. Van Allen.

The <u>control</u> of outer space, basically a military matter, involves many troublesome questions of international law. The problem of the vertical extent of national sovereignty has yet to be determined. It appears to depend on the capability of any nation to deny access to space above its territory by physical means. ~~As far as can be determined,~~ No body of international law yet exists covering

the use of outer space. As a matter of fact, no acceptable definition has yet been evolved as to where "air-space" and "outer-space" begin and end. Maritime law has no such problem because, under most conditions, one is either afloat or ashore. The limits of the "high seas" have been determined by international agreement on the basis of very easily made physical measurements. With respect to outer space, however, such questions are wide open (a discussion of these problems is to be found in our files in papers on the subject by Professor John Cobb Cooper and others.)

The control of radio-communications in our upper atmosphere and in space is another problem which must be settled by international agreement if a completely chaotic condition is to be avoided. Within the next ten years the probabilities are that dozens, if not hundreds, of objects will be in orbit around the earth. Apart from the question of sorting scientific intelligence from this "celestial junkyard" it will be highly important from a military point of view to be able to distinguish an incoming ICBM from other less lethal objects.

By any standards of comparison, the problems involved are tremendous and the programs which must be undertaken in their solution will be lengthy and costly. The technical feasibility studies and the forecasts that have been made by Doctors Purcell, York and others, anticipate the development of such items as booster rockets of one million to five million pounds thrust in a period of 15 to 25 years. It is estimated that such development programs, quite apart from the missile requirement of the military, may cost anywhere from 500 million to a billion a year. We are, therefore, considering something of the general order of magnitude of the AEC. Obviously the Bureau of the Budget will exert an important influence in deciding whether the national economy can stand such a drain for such purposes.

General Organizational Requirements

In considering the proper organization to handle a project of such magnitude two factors must be taken into consideration, - first, how to get the program off the ground immediately, ie. how to get something started now with the facilities that are presently available and, second, how to gear-up for a long-range program to take care of the 5-10-25 year development. This leads to the thought that some sort of Ad Hoc organization could be set up in a very short time, possibly by Executive Order of the President, to take care of the immediate requirements. Such a group would not only act as a temporary operating organization but would also initiate studies that would lead toward a more permanent organization on some basis that could be agreed upon by all departments of government and for which the necessary enabling legislature could be obtained.

Whatever plan is adopted, either for the short or for the long-range period, it would appear that certain basic characteristics should be incorporated. First of all, for reasons stated above, it should be a <u>civilian managed</u> organization both at the policy and at the operating levels. It must have wide contractual powers, and it must be free from the limitations of the Civil Service in hiring personnel. It must have access to, and be able to draw upon, all existing scientific talent in the country, both within government, and without, and it must be able to utilize the physical facilities that already exist in industry, universities, government laboratories and military installations. It must be able to purchase whatever hardware, systems or components it needs from all available sources. It must have its own physical facilities for testing completed vehicles and it must also be empowered to operate airborne and space vehicles.

Possible Organizational Patterns.

To date four specific proposals have been made as to possible organizations to accomplish these ends. These include:

1. the formation of an entirely new agency of government;
2. assignment of the project to the AEC;
3. establishment of the NACA as the controlling agency, with assistance from National Science Foundation, National Academy of Sciences, the military services, etc.
4. assignment of the project to the Advanced Research Projects Agency of the Department of Defense (ARPA).

In the following paragraphs some of the advantages and disadvantages of the above suggestions will be briefly noted.

1. <u>New Agency</u>

The establishment of a wholly new agency may prove to be the eventual solution to the problem. Such an agency should report directly to the Executive Office of the President. It should be empowered by law to perform all the functions stated above and be given the necessary funds to accomplish them.

- 3 -

The major difficulty would be in the time required to establish such an agency. New legislation would be required which might involve a very long time to debate and to formulate. It would need a new staff both on the management and on the scientific sides. This would take a long time to recruit, and in view of the overall shortage of scientific personnel in the country, would draw off key people from other necessary jobs. This procedure would also take a long time.

It would also need new facilities, with the inevitable delays in reaching decisions as to what was needed and where new laboratories should be located, before the planning and construction phases could begin.

In summary, the establishment of a new agency would require a very great legislative effort and a very long time to get into operation.

2. Atomic Energy Commission

Strong Congressional support is in evidence for assigning the mission to the AEC.

There is no question but that the AEC is organizationally sound and is a going concern. It already has the necessary authorization to contract for anything it needs and also is free from civil service restraint in hiring people. Its scope could very easily be expanded so that it could legally perform any additional assignment.

On the other hand, the technology of flight both in and out of the atmosphere is not a part of the normal AEC area of competence. Although it is true that nuclear propulsion for aerial and space vehicles comes within its field, consensus seems to be that practical utilization of such propulsion is 5 to 10 years away. AEC, therefore, has an interest in a very small part of the space exploitation picture but it has had little experience in such matters as high speed aerodynamics, control, guidance, structures, telecommunications, etc.

Furthermore, the AEC is already engaged in a huge operation of great national importance. If it were asked to undertake an additional program of the magnitude contemplated for space exploration, its efforts in each one might be so diluted that long delays in the production of end items would be inevitable and its overall effectiveness seriously impaired.

Although the AEC has unquestionably adequate management and all the authority it would need, it would be required to expand both its facilities and its staff into wholly new technical areas if it were given the space exploitation job.

3. *National Advisory Committee for Aeronautics*

Persuasive arguments can be made for assigning the responsibility for space exploration to the NACA. The Committee itself has suggested that with the support of the National Science Foundation and the National Academy of Sciences it would undertake the job by expanding its facilities.

The NACA is basically a civilian-operated, independent government agency. It has a long history of accomplishment. Its relations with the Congress and with the Executive Departments are good and it has an international standing for competence in scientific fields.

The NACA has been in the space exploitation field for a long time. Most of the work that has been done in extremely high altitude and high speed aerodynamics on which the design of missiles and rockets has been based has been done in its laboratories. It has already made great progress in research in some of the very sophisticated propulsion systems required for space flight. It has recently established a special sub-committee in space flight technology made up of outstanding scientists in the field. Extending its interests into space technology would appear to be a logical evolutionary step from its research activities of the past 40-odd years.

The NACA budget for the coming year is of the order of 80 million and it has been authorized to expand its present personnel of 8,000 to 9,000. Its three laboratories (Langley, Ames and Lewis) and its missile firing range at Wallop's Island represent an aggregate investment of about 350 million dollars.

It has been argued that the difference between the size of current NACA operation and the proposed operation is so great that the result would be, in effect, the establishment of a wholly new agency to which the NACA would be attached. There is no reason to believe, however, given proper authority and adequate funds, that the NACA could not expand its management functions to handle the larger assignment effectively as it did in 1942 to meet the comparably tremendous demands of World War II.

A moderate amount of legislation would be needed to assign the job to NACA. Its contractual authorization would have to be expanded, and the present civil service limitations on personnel would have to be relieved.

4. <u>ARPA</u> - <u>Department of Defense</u>

A strong case can be made for integration of the space program into the Department of Defense under ARPA on the grounds of immediate action. A great deal of hardware is already available, essential facilities (e.g. JPL, ABMA) exist. The facilities are well staffed and the experience level is high.

It has been suggested that whatever form of organization is agreed upon to initiate the space exploration program it should be attached temporarily to ARPA. If this were done it would appear to be important that some provision be made so that the entire outfit could be detached and assigned to some other agency in the future if it subsequently appeared desirable. It might happen that military interests might outweigh the purely scientific and civil aspects to the detriment of the latter. It would be difficult to avoid security restrictions, and participation in international programs of a purely scientific nature might thereby be hampered.

Under its present directive it seems that ARPA could take on the job with a minimum of additional legislation.

<u>Suggested Compromise Program</u>

Of the four proposals discussed above, No. 2, - i.e. assigning the project to the AEC, seems the least practical. As an example of appropriate organization and good management it deserves careful study, but the problems under discussion here seem somewhat outside its main fields of interest.

None of the other proposals would satisfy <u>all</u> the requirements in themselves. A possible compromise suggests itself which might satisfy the requirement for immediate action and also lay the groundwork both as the organization and legislation for future action.

This consists, in effect, of the immediate establishment of a provisional Space Exploration Control Group headed by a special assistant to the President and composed of the operating heads of the several government agencies who are already involved in research, development or operation of space vehicles. Several outstanding individuals from non-government organizations might also be included, but the total group should not be large. Their main function would be the implementation of national space policy as determined by the President and Congress, utilizing all assets and facilities which already exist in established government agencies and in industry. Their secondary function should be the determination of the kind of agency which should be established to put space exploitation on a permanent basis to handle the requests of the foreseeable future.

The suggested procedure might be outlined as follows:

A. <u>Short Range - By Executive Order for Immediate Action</u>

1. Appoint a <u>Special Assistant to the President for Space Exploitation</u>   (This should be the <u>Chairman of the NACA -</u> See Footnote) *

   [handwritten: not a good word? Exploration]

2. Appoint a <u>Provisional Board of Regents for Space Exploitation</u> consisting of: *[handwritten: Director]*

   a. Special Asst. to President for S.E. (Chairman)
   b. ~~Scientific Advisor to President~~
   c. ~~Chairman~~, AEC
   d. Director, NACA
   e. President, NSF
   f. President, NAS
   g. Director, ARPA
   h. Two ~~outstanding~~ civilians, possibly from industry

3. Empower above to   *[handwritten: Technical]*

   a. Establish immediate space objectives
   b. Establish program priorities
   c. Coordinate programs of associated agencies toward meeting established objectives
   d. Utilize funds already appropriated to the associated agencies to implement immediate objectives.

4. Instruct Special Assistant for Space Exploitation to make immediate plans for the establishment of a Permanent Space Exploitation Agency and to prepare the necessary legislation.

B. <u>Long Range - By Legislation for Continuing Action</u>

   1. Organize a permanent <u>Space Exploitation Agency</u>

   2. Authorize the Agency to:

        a. establish, maintain and operate its own testing and operational facilities
        b. enter into whatever contractual arrangements may be necessary with government and civilian agencies
        c. hire personnel without regard to Civil Service restrictions
        d. operate air/space Vehicles

Document 5

Title: James R. Killian, Jr., Special Assistant for Science and Technology; Percival Brundage, Director, Bureau of the Budget; and Nelson A. Rockefeller, Chairman, President's Advisory Committee on Government Organization, Memorandum for the President, "Organization for Civil Space Programs," March 5, 1958, with attached: "Summary of Advantages and Disadvantages of Alternative Organizational Arrangements."

Source: Dwight D. Eisenhower Papers, Eisenhower Library, Abilene, Kansas.

As the three preceding documents have shown, there was substantial attention given within the Executive Office of the President during the December 1957–March 1958 period on how best to organize the nation's space effort. This memorandum was the culmination of that attention and laid the basis for President Eisenhower's decision to create a new civilian space agency.

EXECUTIVE OFFICE OF THE PRESIDENT

PRESIDENT'S ADVISORY COMMITTEE ON GOVERNMENT ORGANIZATION

WASHINGTON 25, D. C.

March 5, 1958

MEMORANDUM FOR THE PRESIDENT

SUBJECT: Organization for Civil Space Programs

<u>The Problem</u>

As you know, there will soon be presented for your consideration civil space programs for the United States which will entail increased expenditures and the employment of important numbers of scientists, engineers and technicians. 1/

This Committee, in conjunction with the Director of the Bureau of the Budget and your Special Assistant for Science and Technology, have given consideration to the manner in which the executive branch should be organized to conduct the new program. This memorandum contains our joint findings and recommendations. The memorandum (1) discusses some of the factors which should be taken into account in establishing the government's organization for these civil space programs, (2) recommends a pattern of organization, and (3) indicates certain interim actions which will be necessary. Also attached is a summary of the advantages and disadvantages of certain alternative organizational arrangements.

1/ These programs do not include those projects relating to space vehicles and exploration which will be carried out in the Department of Defense under the direction of the Advanced Research Projects Agency (ARPA).

- 2 -

Discussions to date suggest that an aggressive space program will produce important civilian gains in the form of advances in general scientific knowledge and the protection of the international prestige of the United States. These benefits will be in addition to such military uses of outer space as may prove feasible.

Establishing a Long Term Organization

Because of the importance of the civil interest in space exploration, the long term organization for Federal programs in this area should be under civilian control. Such civilian domination is also suggested by public and foreign relations considerations. However, civilian control does not envisage taking out from military control projects relating to missiles, anti-missile defense, reconnaissance satellites, military communications, and other space technology relating to weapons systems or direct military requirements.

- 3 -

We have considered a number of different approaches to civil space organization. It is our conclusion that one of these alternatives provides a workable solution to the problem. The other principal alternatives have serious shortcomings which argue against their selection as a basis for space organization.

Recommendation No. 1. We recommend that leadership of the civil space effort be lodged in a strengthened and redesignated National Advisory Committee for Aeronautics.

The National Advisory Committee for Aeronautics (NACA), in a resolution adopted on January 16, 1958, has proposed that the national space program be implemented by the cooperative effort of the Department of Defense, the NACA, the National Academy of Sciences and the National Science Foundation, together with the universities, research institutions, and industrial companies of the nation. NACA further recommended that the development of space vehicles and the operations required for scientific research in space phenomena and space technology be conducted by the NACA when within its capabilities. NACA is now formulating a program which is expected to propose expansion of existing programs and the addition of supplementary research facilities.

- 4 -

Factors Favoring NACA as the Principal Civil Space Agency

1. NACA is a going Federal research agency with a large scientific and engineering staff (approximately 2,000 of its 7,500 employees are in these categories) and a large plant ($300,000,000 in laboratories and test facilities). It can expand its research program and increase its emphasis on space matters with a minimum of delay and can provide a functioning institutional setting for this activity.

2. NACA's aeronautical research has been progressively involving it in technical problems associated with space flight and its current facilities construction program is designed to be useful in space research. It has done research in rocket engines (including advanced chemical propellants), it has developed materials and designs to withstand the thermal effects of high speeds in or on entering the earth's atmosphere, it conducts multi-stage rocket launchings, and in the X-15 project it has taken the leadership (in cooperation with the Navy and Air Force) in developing a manned vehicle capable of flights beyond the earth's atmosphere.

- 5 -

3. If NACA is not given the leading responsibility for the civil space program, its future research role will be limited to aircraft and missiles. Some of its present activities would have to be curtailed, and the logical paths of progress in much of its current work would be closed. It would, under such circumstances, be difficult for NACA to attract and retain the most imaginative and competent scientific and engineering personnel, and all aspects of its mission could suffer. Moreover, it is questionable whether it would be possible to define practicable boundaries between the missile and high performance aircraft research now performed by NACA and the space vehicle projects.

4. NACA has a long history of close and cordial cooperation with the military departments. This cooperation has taken place under a variety of arrangements, usually with little in the way of formalized agreements. Although new relationship problems are bound to arise from an augmented NACA role in space programs, the tradition of comity and civil-military accommodation which has been built up over the years will be a great asset in minimizing friction between the civilian space agency and the Department of Defense.

- 6 -

5. Although much of its work has been done for the military departments, NACA is a civilian agency and is widely recognized as such. A civilian setting for space programs is desirable, and NACA satisfies this requirement.

6. Some of the principal problems in using NACA, as listed below, can be overcome by relatively limited amendments to existing law and by appropriate administrative action. These measures are described in later paragraphs.

Problems in Using NACA as the Agency with Primary Responsibility for Civil Space Programs

1. NACA has in the past been concerned chiefly with research involving air breathing aircraft and missiles. NACA's competence in certain fields related to space flight (such as electronics and space medicine) will need to be augmented. NACA has also had little experience in the direct administration of large scale developmental contracts.

2. Many of the scientists who have done the most work on rocket engines and space vehicles are now employed by Defense Department agencies and by private contractors of the military services. Some means of utilizing such experienced personnel will have to be found which does not unduly impair the capacity of the Department of Defense to continue defense related aspects of missile and space activity.

- 7 -

3. The NACA is not in a position to push ahead with the immediate demonstration projects which may be necessary to protect the nation's world prestige. Therefore the military services may have to be relied on for such demonstrations while NACA is equipping itself for the full performance of the space job.

4. NACA suffers from some of the limitations imposed on civil service agencies, and some scientists are known to favor reliance on private research organizations operating under government contracts. Ceilings and numerical restrictions on the salaries of top scientific staff and the general lag in Classification Act salaries are among the obstacles to administration through government laboratories which pose problems in utilizing NACA.

5. NACA now spends around $100,000,000 per year. A civil space program may eventually entail additional annual expenditures substantially in excess of this amount. It is obvious that important changes in NACA will be required by such an expansion, and the agency may have some difficulty in assimilating the additional staff and functions.

- 8 -

<u>Recommendation No. 2.</u> <u>We recommend that NACA's basic law be amended to give NACA the authority and flexibility to overcome or mitigate the problems noted above so that NACA can carry out its total program effectively.</u>

Specifically the amendments should:

a. Rename the NACA the National Aeronautical and Space Agency to get away from the limited connotations of the term "aeronautics" when used alone and to recognize that NACA has long since ceased to be an "advisory committee" as the term is customarily used.

b. Retain a board for top policy direction. Some changes in the composition of the present NACA board may be appropriate.

c. Provide for the appointment of a Director by the President by and with the advice and consent of the Senate.

d. Provide a system for the fixing of compensation of employees which, under appropriate Presidential controls, will permit the agency to pay rates which are reasonably competitive with the rates paid by non-Federal employers for comparable work. (This amendment will ease the salary limitations under the Classification Act of 1949 which have caused so much concern in and out of NACA.)

- 9 -

Certain additional miscellaneous powers may also have to be given NACA if further investigation reveals that they are not already available and confirms that they will be of material assistance to the agency.

The above powers would give NACA as much flexibility as can reasonably be achieved by contract laboratories and would at the same time permit retention of the traditional NACA practice of conducting such research and testing through its own government employee staffed facilities as it determines to be desirable in carrying out a space program.

There will remain the need to refine relationships with the Department of Defense in space matters and to draw upon and utilize staff and experience now lodged in the laboratories of the military services and their contractors, but the reorganized NACA would be equipped to work out these problems in a flexible manner. Some Presidential intervention may prove necessary to bring about or implement agreements between the space agency and Defense, and it may also be desirable for the President to be given the specific authority to transfer to NACA space activities directly related to the civil program which are now being performed by other agencies.

- 10 -

Overlapping between NACA's civil space program and the work of Defense on military projects should be kept to a minimum. This can be done if Defense, in a manner analogous to the practice followed on developing aircraft and missiles, makes appropriate use of NACA for supporting research and development on military space vehicles. An arrangement of this kind could reduce duplication without undermining the basic Defense Department responsibility for developing weapons systems and other military equipment.

Interim Measures

Recommendation No. 3. If you approve our recommended approach to space organization, we further recommend that a number of interim and short-term measures be given immediate attention.

Specifically, we propose:

a. An all-out attempt should be made to draft needed legislation within the next few weeks so that there will be some chance of final action during the current session of the Congress. At the same time decisions should be made with respect to the supplemental appropriations which will be required for NACA to get its part of the space program under way. If congressional action

- 11 -

can be secured on both matters before adjournment, the full civil space program under arrangements designed to serve long term needs can be launched this year.

If it proves impossible to obtain the enactment of the comprehensive legislation strengthening NACA during the current session, the passage of the general Classification Act revisions now pending, the authorization of additional super-grade and Public Law 313 positions, and the securing of supplemental appropriations would still enable NACA to get under way with a space program.

b. While awaiting congressional action we suggest that the President advise the NACA's top committee that it is being charged with the responsibility for developing and arranging for the execution of the civil space program. NACA will at first have to rely heavily upon the Department of Defense and its instrumentalities for interim development and demonstration projects. However, the problems created by such arrangements will be minimized once the President gives NACA the clear-cut authority required for it to select and monitor the advanced space projects entrusted to the Department of Defense during the transitional period.

- 12 -

    c. None of the immediate measures is more essential and fundamental than defining as clearly as possible just what the nation plans to do in the space field. At the same time an effort must be made to estimate with reasonable exactness the annual additional costs of the civil space program.

Immediate Action

If you concur in the recommendations set forth above, the Director of the Bureau of the Budget will proceed, in cooperation with this Committee, your Special Assistant for Science and Technology and other departments and agencies concerned, to develop for your consideration specific proposals for legislative and executive action.

James R. Killian, Jr., Special Assistant for Science and Technology	Percival Brundage, Director, Bureau of the Budget	Nelson A. Rockefeller, Chairman

Attachment

Summary of Advantages and Disadvantages of Alternative Organizational Arrangements

1. Use of a private contractor to carry out the civil space program under supervision of NACA.

A variation of our recommended organizational approach is to select NACA as the civilian agency to supervise contracts with a private laboratory charged with developing and testing space vehicles. This is the pattern followed by the Atomic Energy Commission in much of its research. This approach has also been used to some extent by the military services in developing missiles.

Advantages

Contract operation is preferred by some scientific personnel as a means of circumventing government salary and administrative controls. It would retain NACA in a supervisory capacity while making use of selected private research organizations.

Disadvantages

This approach is in conflict with the traditional NACA practice of carrying out research largely through its own government-employee staffed laboratories; there is no assurance that a private research laboratory can be found to do the work on a sufficiently urgent schedule; and such greater flexibility as private laboratories may enjoy can also be provided NACA through the changes in law previously described.

- 2 -

Conclusion

No real gains would flow from this alternative which could not be achieved under the preferred organization. It would be better to permit NACA to make its own decisions as to the extent to which it would use contracting authority in executing the space research program. It is assumed, of course, that NACA will, in fact, make fairly extensive use of research contracts, but on a selective basis.

2. Utilization of the Department of Defense

The recent Supplemental Military Construction Authorization Act authorizes the Secretary of Defense, for a period of one year, to carry on such space projects as may be designated by the President. It confers permanent authority for the Secretary or his designee to proceed with missile and other space projects directly related to weapons systems and military requirements.

Advantages

The Department of Defense is now doing most of the current missile and satellite work; it has the bulk of the scientists and engineers active in these fields in its employ or on the rolls of its contractors; it will have to continue work on space vehicles on an interim basis for demonstration purposes; it is experienced in working with and utilizing the facilities of NACA; and it may be possible for a civilian agency of the Department to carry out the program.

- 3 -

Disadvantages

The Department of Defense is a military agency in law and in the eyes of the world and placing the space program under it would be interpreted as emphasizing military goals; the space program is expected to produce benefits largely unrelated to the central mission of the Department of Defense; there is some danger that the non-military phases of space activity would be neglected; the Department is already so overloaded with its central military responsibilities that care should be taken to avoid charging it with additional civil functions; cooperation with other nations in international civil space matters could be made more difficult; and adequate civil-military cooperation can be achieved under the recommended organization without assigning inappropriate functions to Defense.

Conclusion

Since the space program has a relatively limited military significance, at least for the foreseeable future, and since the general scientific objectives should not be subordinated to military priorities, it is essential that the arrangements for space organization provide for leadership by a civilian agency.

- 4 -

3. <u>Utilization of the Atomic Energy Commission</u>

There are now pending before the Congress bills which would authorize the Atomic Energy Commission to proceed with the development of vehicles for the exploration of outer space. Among these bills are S. 3117 (introduced by Senator Anderson) and S. 3000 (introduced by Senator Gore). The justification for these proposals is the role already being played by the Atomic Energy Commission in developing nuclear propelled jet and rocket engines.

<u>Advantages</u>

The Atomic Energy Commission is a civilian agency with competence in directing scientific research and development projects; it has had experience in managing research contracts and in working with the military agencies; and it is now charged with developing a nuclear rocket engine which may eventually be used to propel space vehicles.

<u>Disadvantages</u>

The Atomic Energy Commission is concerned chiefly with the use of a single form of energy and it is expected that chemical propellants, not atomic energy, will be the chief power source for space vehicles for years to come. Moreover, the Commission has virtually no experience or competence in most aspects of the design, construction and testing of space vehicles.

Conclusion

The Atomic Energy Commission has a contribution to make in the space field. However, it should limit its work to the aspects of the space problem in which nuclear energy may have practical applications. An administration position along these lines has already been conveyed to the Chairman of the Atomic Energy Commission.

4. Creation of a Department of Science and Technology

Senators Humphrey, McClellan and Yarborough recently introduce S. 3126, a bill to create a Department of Science and Technology. The bill calls for the establishment of a new executive department which at the outset would contain or be given the functions of the National Science Foundation, the Patent Office, the Office of Technical Services of the Department of Commerce, the National Bureau of Standards, the Atomic Energy Commission and certain divisions of the Smithsonian Institution. The Secretary would also be authorized to establish institutes for basic research.

Advantages

The proposed department would provide a civilian setting for the administration of space programs, and it would give this and other scientific activities the prestige and accessibility to the President associated with departmental status.

Disadvantages

The proposed department will be highly controversial, and there is no assurance that it can be established in time to assume the responsibility for civil space programs. It is also unlikely that science, of itself, will provide a sound basis for organizing an executive department.

Conclusion

There would be little prospect of getting such a reorganization approved and functioning in the near future. Even if the department could be created, it might not provide as good a setting for a high priority space program as that proposed under the preferred organization.

Document 6

Title: The President's Science Advisory Committee, "Introduction to Outer Space," March 26, 1958.

Source: NASA Historical Reference Collection, NASA History Office, NASA Headquarters, Washington, D.C.

An initial assignment for the President's Science Advisory Committee, which was formed in the aftermath of the launches of Sputniks I and II, was to assess the appropriate direction and pace for the U.S. space program. This committee focused heavily on the scientific aspects of the space program. With President Eisenhower's endorsement, on March 26, 1958, the committee released a report outlining the importance of space activities, but it recommended a cautiously measured pace.

NASA's Origins and the Dawn of the Space Age

INTRODUCTION TO OUTER SPACE

THE WHITE HOUSE
March 26, 1958

**A STATEMENT
BY THE PRESIDENT**

AND

INTRODUCTION TO OUTER SPACE

**AN EXPLANATORY STATEMENT
PREPARED BY
THE PRESIDENT'S
SCIENCE ADVISORY COMMITTEE**

STATEMENT

BY THE PRESIDENT

IN CONNECTION with a study of space science and technology made at my request, the President's Science Advisory Committee, of which Dr. James R. Killian is Chairman, has prepared a brief "Introduction to Outer Space" for the nontechnical reader.

This is not science fiction. This is a sober, realistic presentation prepared by leading scientists.

I have found this statement so informative and interesting that I wish to share it with all the people of America, and indeed with all the people of the earth. I hope that it can be widely disseminated by all news media for it clarifies many aspects of space and space technology in a way which can be helpful to all people as the United States proceeds with its peaceful program in space science and exploration. Every person has the opportunity to share through understanding in the adventures which lie ahead.

This statement of the Science Advisory Committee makes clear the opportunities which a developing space technology can provide to extend man's knowledge of the earth, the solar system, and the universe. These opportunities reinforce my conviction that we and other nations have a great responsibility to promote the peaceful use of space and to utilize the new knowledge obtainable from space science and technology for the benefit of all mankind.

Dwight D. Eisenhower

INTRODUCTION TO OUTER SPACE

AN EXPLANATORY STATEMENT
PREPARED BY
THE PRESIDENT'S
SCIENCE ADVISORY COMMITTEE

WHAT ARE THE principal reasons for undertaking a national space program? What can we expect to gain from space science and exploration? What are the scientific laws and facts and the technological means which it would be helpful to know and understand in reaching sound policy decisions for a United States space program and its management by the Federal Government? This statement seeks to provide brief and introductory answers to these questions.

It is useful to distinguish among four factors which give importance, urgency, and inevitability to the advancement of space technology.

The first of these factors is the compelling urge of man to explore and to discover, the thrust of curiosity that leads men to try to go where no one has gone before. Most of the surface of the earth has now been explored and men now turn to the exploration of outer space as their next objective.

Second, there is the defense objective for the development of space technology. We wish to be sure that space is not used to endanger our security. If space is to be used for military purposes, we must be prepared to use space to defend ourselves.

Third, there is the factor of national prestige. To be strong and bold in space technology will enhance the prestige of the United States among the peoples of the world and create added confidence in our scientific, technological, industrial, and military strength.

Fourth, space technology affords new opportunities for scientific observation and experiment which will add to our knowledge and understanding of the earth, the solar system, and the universe.

The determination of what our space program should be must take into consideration all four of these objectives. While this statement deals mainly with the use of space for scientific inquiry, we fully recognize the importance of the other three objectives.

In fact it has been the military quest for ultra long-range rockets that has provided man with new machinery so powerful that it can readily put satellites in orbit, and, before long, send instruments out to explore the moon and nearby planets. In this way, what was at first a purely military enterprise has opened up an exciting era of exploration that few men, even a decade ago, dreamed would come in this century.

WHY SATELLITES STAY UP

The basic laws governing satellites and space flight are fascinating in their own right. And while they have been well known to scientists ever since Newton, they may still seem a little puzzling and unreal to many of us. Our children, however, will understand them quite well.

We all know that the harder you throw a stone the farther it will travel before falling to earth. If you could imagine your strength so fantastically multiplied that you could throw a stone at a speed of 15,000 m. p. h., it would travel a great distance. It would, in fact, easily cross the Atlantic Ocean before the earth's gravity pulled it down. Now imagine being able to throw the stone just a little faster, say about 18,000 m. p. h., what would happen then?

The stone would again cross the ocean, but this time it would travel much farther than it did before. It would travel so far that it would overshoot the earth, so to speak, and keep falling until it was back where it started. Since in this imaginary example there is no atmospheric resistance to slow the stone down, it would still be travelling at the original speed, 18,000 m. p. h., when it had got back to its starting point. So around the earth it goes again. From the stone's point of view, it is continuously falling, except that its very slight downward arc exactly matches the curvature of the earth, and so it stays aloft—or as the scientist would say, "in orbit"—indefinitely.

Since the earth has an atmosphere, of course, neither stones nor satellites can be sent whizzing around the earth at tree-top level. Satellites must first be lifted beyond the reach of atmospheric resistance. It is absence of atmospheric resistance plus speed that makes the satellite possible. It may seem odd that weight or mass has nothing to do with a satellite's orbit. If a feather were released from a 10-ton satellite, the two would stay together, following the same path in the airless void. There is, however, a slight vestige of atmosphere even a few hundred miles above the earth, and its resistance will cause the feather to spiral inward toward the earth sooner than the satellite. It is atmospheric resistance, however slight, that has set limits on the life of all satellites launched to date. Beyond a few hundred miles the remaining trace of atmosphere fades away so rapidly that tomorrow's satellites should stay aloft thousands of years, and, perhaps, indefinitely. The higher the satellite, incidentally, the less speed it needs to stay in orbit once it gets there (thus, the moon's speed is only a little more than 2,000 m. p. h.), but to launch a satellite toward a more distant orbit requires a higher initial speed and greater expenditure of energy.

THE THRUST INTO SPACE

Rocket engineers rate rockets not in horsepower, but in thrust. Thrust is just another name for push, and it is expressed in pounds of force. The rocket gets its thrust or push by exhausting material backward. It is this thrust that lifts the rocket off the earth and accelerates it, making it move faster and faster.

As everyone knows, it is more difficult to accelerate an automobile than a baby carriage. To place satellites weighing 1,000 to 2,000 pounds in orbit requires a first-stage rocket, engine, or engines, having a thrust in the neighborhood of 200,000 to 400,000 pounds. Rocket engines able to supply this thrust have been under development for some time. For launching a satellite, or other space vehicle, the rocket engineer divides his rockets into two, three, or more stages, which can be dropped one after the other in flight, thus reducing the total weight that must be accelerated to the final velocity desired. (In other words, it is a great waste of energy to lift one huge fuel tank into orbit when the tank can be divided into smaller tanks—each packaged in its own stage with its own rocket motor—that can be left behind as they become empty.)

To launch some of the present satellites has required rockets weighing up to 1,000 times the weight of the satellite itself. But it will be possible to reduce takeoff weights until they are only 50 to 100 times that of the satellite. The rocket's high ratio of gross weight to payload follows from a fundamental limitation in the exhaust velocities that can be achieved by chemical propellants.

If we want to send up not a satellite but a device that will reach the moon, we need a larger rocket relative to its payload in order that the final stage can be accelerated to about 25,000 m. p. h. This speed, called the "escape velocity," is the speed with which a projectile must be thrown to escape altogether from the gravitational pull of the earth. If a rocket fired at the moon is to use as little fuel as possible, it must attain the escape velocity very near the beginning of its trip. After this peak speed is reached, the rocket will be gradually slowed down by the earth's pull, but it will still move fast enough to reach the moon in 2 or 3 days.

THE MOON AS A GOAL

Moon exploration will involve three distinct levels of difficulty. The first would be a simple shot at the moon, ending either in a "hard" landing or a circling of the moon. Next in difficulty would be a "soft" landing. And most difficult of all would be a "soft" landing followed by a safe return to earth.

The payload for a simple moon shot might be a small instrument carrier similar to a satellite. For the more difficult "soft" landing, the carrier would have to include, as part of its payload, a "retro-rocket" (a *de*celerating rocket) to provide braking action, since the moon has no atmosphere that could serve as a cushion.

To carry out the most difficult feat, a round trip to the moon, will require that the initial payload include not only "retro-rockets" but rockets to take off again from the moon. Equipment will also be required aboard to get the payload through the atmosphere and safely back to earth. To land a man on the moon and get him home safely again will require a very big rocket engine indeed—one with a thrust in the neighborhood of one or two million pounds. While nuclear power may prove superior to chemical fuels in engines of multi-million-pound thrust, even the atom will provide no short cut to space exploration.

Sending a small instrument carrier to Mars, although not requiring much more initial propulsion than a simple moon shot, would take a much longer travel time (8 months or more), and the problems of navigation and final guidance are formidable.

A MESSAGE FROM MARS

Fortunately, the exploration of the moon and nearby planets need not be held up for lack of rocket engines big enough to send men and instrument carriers out into space and home again. Much that scientists wish to learn from satellites and space voyages into the solar system can be gathered by instruments and transmitted back to earth. This transmission, it turns out, is relatively easy with today's rugged and tiny electronic equipment.

For example, a transmitter with a power of just one or two watts can easily radio information from the moon to the earth. And messages from Mars, on the average some 50 million to 100 million miles away at the time the rocket would arrive, can be transmitted to earth with less power than that used by most commercial broadcasting stations. In some ways, indeed, it appears that it will be easier to send a clear radio message between Mars and earth than between New York and Tokyo.

This all leads up to an important point about space exploration. The cost of transporting men and material through space will be extremely high, but the cost and difficulty of sending *information* through space will be comparatively low.

WILL THE RESULTS JUSTIFY THE COSTS?

Since the rocket power plants for space exploration are already in existence or being developed for military need, the cost of additional scientific research, using these rockets, need not be exorbitant. Still, the cost will not be small, either. This raises an important question that scientists and the general public (which will pay the bill) both must face: Since there are still so many unanswered scientific questions and problems all around us on earth, why should we start asking new questions and seeking out new problems in space? How can the results possibly justify the cost?

Scientific research, of course, has never been amenable to rigorous cost accounting in advance. Nor, for that matter, has exploration of any sort. But if we have learned one lesson, it is that research and exploration have a remarkable way of paying off—quite apart from the fact that they demonstrate that man is alive and insatiably curious. And we all feel richer for knowing what explorers and scientists have learned about the universe in which we live.

It is in these terms that we must measure the value of launching satellites and sending rockets into space. These ventures may have practical utility, some of which will be noted later. But the scientific questions come first.

THE VIEW FROM A SATELLITE

Here are some of the things that scientists say can be done with the new satellites and other space mechanisms. A satellite in orbit can do three things: (1) It can sample the strange new environment through which it moves; (2) it can look down and see the earth as it has never been seen before; and (3) it can look out into the universe and record information that can never reach the earth's surface because of the intervening atmosphere.

The satellite's immediate environment at the edge of space is empty only by earthly standards. Actually, "empty" space is rich in energy, radiation, and fast-moving particles of great variety. Here we will be exploring the active medium, a kind of electrified plasma, dominated by the sun, through which our earth moves. Scientists have indirect evidence that there are vast systems of magnetic fields and electric currents that are connected somehow with the outward flow of charged material from the sun. These fields and currents the satellites will be able to measure for the first time. Also for the first time, the satellites will give us a detailed three-dimensional picture of the earth's gravity and its magnetic field.

Physicists are anxious to run one crucial and fairly simple gravity experiment as soon as possible. This experiment will test an important prediction made by Einstein's General Theory of Relativity, namely, that a clock will run faster as the gravitational field around it is reduced. If one of the fantastically accurate clocks, using atomic frequencies, were placed in a satellite and should run faster than its counterpart on earth, another of Einstein's great and daring predictions would be confirmed. (This is not the same as the prediction that any moving clock will appear to a stationary observer to lose time—a prediction that physicists already regard as well confirmed.)

There are also some special questions about cosmic rays which can be settled only by detecting the rays before they shatter themselves against the earth's atmosphere. And, of course, animals carried in satellites will begin to answer the question: What is the effect of weightlessness on physiological and psychological functions? (Gravity is not felt inside a satellite because the earth's pull is precisely balanced by centrifugal force. This is just another way of saying that bodies inside a satellite behave exactly as they would inside a freely falling elevator.)

The satellite that will turn its attention downward holds great promise for meteorology and the eventual improvement of weather forecasting. Present weather stations on land and sea can keep only about 10 percent of the atmosphere under surveillance. Two or three weather satellites could make a cloud inventory of the whole globe every few hours. From this inventory meteorologists believe they could spot large storms (including hurricanes) in their early stages and chart their direction of movement with much more accuracy than at present. Other instruments in the satellites will measure for the first time how much solar energy is falling upon the earth's atmosphere and how much is reflected and radiated back into space by clouds, oceans, the continents, and by the great polar ice fields.

It is not generally appreciated that the earth has to send back into space, over the long run, exactly as much heat energy as it receives from the sun. If this were not so the earth would either heat up or cool off. But there is an excess of income over outgo in the tropical regions, and an excess of outgo over income in the polar regions. This imbalance has to be continuously rectified by the activity of the earth's atmosphere which we call weather.

By looking at the atmosphere from the outside, satellites will provide the first real accounting of the energy imbalances, and their consequent tensions, all around the globe. With the insight gained from such studies, meteorologists hope they may improve long-range forecasting of world weather trends.

Finally, there are the satellites that will look not just around or down, but out into space. Carrying ordinary telescopes as well as special instruments for recording X-rays, ultraviolet, and other radiations, these satellites cannot fail to reveal new sights forever hidden from observers who are bound to the earth. What these sights will be, no one can tell. But scientists know that a large part of all stellar radiation lies in the ultraviolet region of the spectrum, and this is totally blocked by the earth's atmosphere. Also blocked are other very long wavelengths of "light" of the kind usually referred to as radio waves. Some of these get through the so-called "radio window" in the atmosphere and can be detected by radio telescopes, but scientists would like a look at the still longer waves that cannot penetrate to earth.

Even those light signals that now reach the earth can be recorded with brilliant new clarity by satellite telescopes. All existing photographs of the moon and nearby planets are smeared by the same turbulence of the atmosphere that makes the stars twinkle. Up above the atmosphere the twinkling will stop and we should be able to see for the first time what Mars really looks like. And we shall want a really sharp view before launching the first rocket to Mars.

A CLOSE-UP OF THE MOON

While these satellite observations are in progress, other rockets will be striking out for the moon with other kinds of instruments. Photographs of the back or hidden side of the moon may prove quite unexciting, or they may reveal some spectacular new feature now unguessed. Of greater scientific interest is the question whether or not the moon has a magnetic field. Since no one knows for sure why the earth has such a field, the presence or absence of one on the moon should throw some light on the mystery.

But what scientists would most like to learn from a close-up study of the moon is something of its origin and history. Was it originally molten? Does it now have a fluid core, similar to the earth's? And just what is the nature of the lunar surface? The answer to these and many other questions should shed light, directly or indirectly, on the origin and history of the earth and the surrounding solar system.

While the moon is believed to be devoid of life, even the simplest and most primitive, this cannot be taken for granted. Some scientists have suggested that small particles with the properties of life—germs or spores—could exist in space and could have drifted on to the moon. If we are to test this intriguing hypothesis we must be careful not to contaminate the moon's surface, in the biological sense, beforehand. There are strong scientific reasons, too, for avoiding radioactive contamination of the moon until its naturally acquired radioactivity can be measured.

. . . AND ON TO MARS

The nearest planets to earth are Mars and Venus. We know quite enough about Mars to suspect that it may support some form of life. To land instrument carriers on Mars and Venus will be easier, in one respect, than achieving a "soft" landing on the moon. The reason is that both planets have atmospheres that can be used to cushion the final approach. These atmospheres might also be used to support balloons equipped to carry out both meteorological soundings and a general photo survey of surface features. The Venusian atmosphere, of course, consists of what appears to be a dense layer of clouds so that its surface has never been seen at all from earth.

Remotely-controlled scientific expeditions to the moon and nearby planets could absorb the energies of scientists for many decades. Since man is such an adventurous creature, there will undoubtedly come a time when he can no longer resist going out and seeing for himself. It would be foolish to try to predict today just when this moment will arrive. It might not arrive in this century, or it might come within one or two decades. So much will depend on how rapidly we want to expand and accelerate our program. According to one rough estimate it might require a total investment of about a couple of billion dollars, spent over a number of years to equip ourselves to land a man on the moon and to return him safely to earth.

THE SATELLITE RADIO NETWORK

Meanwhile, back at earth, satellites will be entering into the everyday affairs of men. Not only will they be aiding the meteorologists, but they could surely—and rather quickly—be pressed into service for expanding world-wide communications, including intercontinental television.

At present all trans-oceanic communication is by cable (which is costly to install) or by shortwave radio (which is easily disrupted by solar storms). Television cannot practically be beamed more than a few hundred miles because the wavelengths needed to carry it will not bend around the earth and will not bounce off the region of the atmosphere known as the ionosphere. To solve this knotty problem, satellites may be the thing, for they can serve as high-flying radio relay stations. Several suitably-equipped and properly-spaced satellites would be able to receive TV signals from any point on the globe and to relay them directly—or perhaps via a second satellite—to any other point. Powered with solar batteries, these relay stations in space should be able to keep working for many years.

MILITARY APPLICATIONS OF SPACE TECHNOLOGY

The development of military rockets has provided the technological base for space exploration. It will probably continue to do so, because of the commanding military importance of the ballistic missile. The subject of ballistic missiles lies outside our present discussion. We ask instead, putting missiles aside, what other military applications of space technology can we see ahead?

There are important, foreseeable, military uses for space vehicles. These lie, broadly speaking, in the fields of *communication* and *reconnaissance*. To this we could add meteorology, for the possible advances in meteorological science which have already been described would have military implications. The use of satellites for radio relay links has also been described, and it does not take much imagination to foresee uses of such techniques in long range military operations.

The reconnaissance capabilities of a satellite are due, of course, to its position high above the earth and the fact that its orbit carries it in a predictable way over much of the globe. Its disadvantage is its necessarily great distance, 200 miles or more, from the surface. A highly magnifying camera or telescope is needed to picture the earth's surface in even moderate detail. To the human eye, from 200 miles away, a football stadium would be a barely distinguishable speck. A telescopic camera can do a good deal better, depending on its size and complexity. It is certainly feasible to obtain reconnaissance information with a fairly elaborate instrument, information which could be relayed back to the earth by radio.

Much has been written about space as a future theater of war, raising such suggestions as satellite bombers, military bases on the moon, and so on. For the most part, even the more sober proposals do not hold up well on close examination or appear to be achievable at an early date. Granted that they will become technologically possible, most of these schemes, nevertheless, appear to be clumsy and ineffective ways of doing a job. Take one example, the satellite as a bomb carrier. A satellite cannot simply drop a bomb. An object released from a satellite doesn't fall. So there is no special advantage in being over the target. Indeed, the only way to "drop" a bomb directly down from a satellite is to carry out aboard the satellite a rocket launching of the magnitude required for an intercontinental missile. A better scheme is to give the weapon to be launched from the satellite a small push, after which it will spiral in gradually. But that means launching it from a moving platform halfway around the world, with every disadvantage compared to a missile base on the ground. In short, the earth would appear to be, after all, the best weapons carrier.

This is only one example; each idea has to be judged on its own merits. There may well be important military applications for space vehicles which we cannot now foresee, and developments in space technology which open up quite novel possibilities. The history of science and technology reminds us sharply of the limitations of our vision. Our road to future strength is the achievement of scientific insight and technical skill by vigorous participation in these new explorations. In this setting, our appropriate military strength will grow naturally and surely.

A SPACE TIMETABLE

Thus we see that satellites and space vehicles can carry out a great variety of scientific missions, and a number of military ones as well.

Indeed, the scientific opportunities are so numerous and so inviting that scientists from many countries will certainly want to participate. Perhaps the International Geophysical Year will suggest a model for the international exploration of space in the years and decades to come.

The timetable on the following page suggests the approximate order in which some of the scientific and technical objectives mentioned in this review may be attained.

The timetable is not broken down into years, since there is yet too much uncertainty about the scale of the effort that will be made. The timetable simply lists various types of space investigations and goals under three broad headings: Early, Later, Still Later.

SCIENTIFIC OBJECTIVES

EARLY
1. Physics
2. Geophysics
3. Meteorology
4. Minimal Moon Contact
5. Experimental Communications
6. Space Physiology

LATER
1. Astronomy
2. Extensive Communications
3. Biology
4. Scientific Lunar Investigation
5. Minimal Planetary Contact
6. Human Flight in Orbit

STILL LATER
1. Automated Lunar Exploration
2. Automated Planetary Exploration
3. Human Lunar Exploration and Return

AND MUCH LATER STILL
Human Planetary Exploration

In conclusion, we venture two observations. Research in outer space affords new opportunities in science, but it does not diminish the importance of science on earth. Many of the secrets of the universe will be fathomed in laboratories on earth, and the progress of our science and technology and the welfare of the Nation require that our regular scientific programs go forward without loss of pace, in fact at an increased pace. It would not be in the national interest to exploit space science at the cost of weakening our efforts in other scientific endeavors. This need not happen if we plan our national program for space science and technology as part of a balanced national effort in all science and technology.

Our second observation is prompted by technical considerations. For the present, the rocketry and other equipment used in space technology must usually be employed at the very limit of its capacity. This means that failures of equipment and uncertainties of schedule are to be expected. It therefore appears wise to be cautious and modest in our predictions and pronouncements about future space activities—and quietly bold in our execution.

Dr. James R. Killian, Jr., *Chairman*
Dr. Robert F. Bacher
Dr. William O. Baker
Dr. Lloyd V. Berkner
Dr. Hans A. Bethe
Dr. Detlev W. Bronk
Dr. James H. Doolittle
Dr. James B. Fisk
Dr. Caryl P. Haskins
Dr. George B. Kistiakowsky
Dr. Edwin H. Land
Dr. Edward M. Purcell
Dr. Isidor I. Rabi
Dr. H. P. Robertson
Dr. Paul A. Weiss
Dr. Jerome B. Wiesner
Dr. Herbert York
Dr. Jerrold R. Zacharias

Document 7

Title: "Main Problems in the Senate Bill Establishing a Federal Space Agency," July 7, 1958.

Source: Ann Whitman File, Dwight D. Eisenhower Diary Series, Eisenhower Library, Abilene, Kansas.

During the evening of July 7, 1958, President Eisenhower met with Senate Majority Leader Lyndon B. Johnson to discuss the legislation to create a national space agency. Bryce Harlow, a congressional liaison aide to Eisenhower who handled defense and space issues, is thought to have drafted this memorandum to prepare Eisenhower for his meeting with Johnson. Ann Whitman was Eisenhower's personal secretary. The notation on the upper right hand corner of the first page probably refers to an unrelated meeting that Eisenhower had earlier in the day with Senator Harry Byrd of Virginia.

MAIN PROBLEMS IN THE SENATE BILL ESTABLISHING A FEDERAL SPACE AGENCY

(a) Creation of a Policy Board;

(b) Transfer of functions

Staff notes offpt Byrd 7/7

THE POLICY BOARD

What it is.

This is a seven member Board in the Executive Office of the President. All seven are Federal officials who, in their principal assignment, have been appointed by the President and confirmed by the Senate. The seven include the Secretaries of State and Defense, the AEC Chairman, and the Director of the new Space Agency. The President names the remaining three to represent other federal agencies interested in aeronautical and space activities.

What it does.

The Board conducts a continuing survey of United States Space matters, recommends a United States program, decides who shall be responsible for major projects, and decides whether any project is in fact an aeronautical and space activity.

Added Features.

The Secretary of Defense is a member, but no other member may be from Defense. The Secretary may appeal Board decisions to the President when he thinks National Security would be adversely affected.

- 2 -

Objections to the Board.

(1) Conflicts with the concept of a single head directly responsible to the President;

(2) Prescribes by statute the manner in which, and the officials through whom, the President will exercise his judgment and responsibility -- including a part of his responsibility as Commander-in-Chief;

(3) Divides responsibility, and makes it difficult to hold anyone accountable for results;

(4) Would encourage Agency logrolling and suppress issues the President should decide;

(5) Denies the President flexibility, while imposing a new chore on agency heads whose full-time jobs may not always bear upon the space problem at hand.

The House Approach.

The House has no such policy board. It followed the President's recommendations for a single civilian head, responsible directly to the President.

The House followed the President's recommendation for a statutory 17-man <u>Advisory</u> Committee (eight from private life, and nine government representatives -- at least three of whom shall be from Defense. Under the Senate bill, there could be advisory committees, but they would lack stature. Hence, they would not attract the kind of scientific talent needed.

Two important drawbacks in the House bill do not appear in the Senate version. The House sets up: (1) A military liaison committee, with a military applications division in the new Agency; and (2) A nuclear liaison committee, with a nuclear applications division. We have urged that these be stricken.

AUTHORITY TO TRANSFER FUNCTIONS

What the bill does.

    The Senate bill has no transfer provisions. The report says reorganization plans should be used where programs or projects are to be transferred to the new Agency.

Problems created by this approach.

    (1) No functions could be moved to the new agency until next April, since reorganization plans must sit before Congress for 60 consecutive days of a session.

    (2) This will hamper the new agency in the first eight months of its existence, and make for duplication of effort within the government.

    (3) It will delay consolidation and obstruct planning, since authority for most Defense space projects expires next February.

    (4) It will involve Congress in the reviewing the placement of very technical scientific programs and projects within the Executive Branch.

NOTE: The House bill parallels the Administration's on the transfer provisions. Functions related primarily to space and aeronautics could be promptly switched to the Space Agency, with the concurrence of the agency giving up the function, and with the approval of the President.

    The House rejected the Reorganization Plan idea, but requires that each House of Congress be notified about every transfer made.

General Points

(1) There is real concern in Congress about protecting the proper role of the military in our space activities. There is no essential difference in the stated purposes of House and Senate sponsors regarding the military. However, the actual language differs. We have taken the position (concurred in by Defense) that we prefer the Senate language. Insofar as it relates to military participation, the Senate language properly protects the responsibilities of the Defense Department.

(2) The Senate bill provides a Joint Congressional Committee, while the House provides two standing committees. The House version, which we endorsed, seems assured.

(3) There are other differences, all minor, relating to such things as patent rights and employee pay provisions.

Document 8

Title: "National Aeronautics and Space Act of 1958," Public Law 85–568, 72 Stat. 426, signed by President Eisenhower on July 29, 1958.

Source: Record Group 255, National Archives and Records Administration, Washington, D.C.

After the launch of Sputnik and the publicity surrounding it, the Eisenhower administration moved quickly to create an American civilian space agency. The National Advisory Committee for Aeronautics (NACA) was too small for the task, however, so the White House decided that a new agency, with the NACA as its core, but also including rocket and space engineers involved in various defense programs, was needed. On March 5, 1958, President Eisenhower approved a final memorandum ordering the Bureau of Budget to draft a space bill immediately. It was ready three weeks later and was sent to Congress on April 2. Senator Lyndon B. Johnson had much influence on the form of the final bill, which was passed after lengthy congressional deliberations. In particular, Congress added to the administration bill a requirement for a National Aeronautics and Space Council as a presidential-level policy coordinating board.

[PUBLIC LAW 85-568]

H. R. 12575

Eighty-fifth Congress of the United States of America

AT THE SECOND SESSION

Begun and held at the City of Washington on Tuesday, the seventh day of January, one thousand nine hundred and fifty-eight

An Act

To provide for research into problems of flight within and outside the earth's atmosphere, and for other purposes.

Be it enacted by the Senate and House of Representatives of the United States of America in Congress assembled,

TITLE I—SHORT TITLE, DECLARATION OF POLICY, AND DEFINITIONS

SHORT TITLE

SEC. 101. This Act may be cited as the "National Aeronautics and Space Act of 1958".

DECLARATION OF POLICY AND PURPOSE

SEC. 102. (a) The Congress hereby declares that it is the policy of the United States that activities in space should be devoted to peaceful purposes for the benefit of all mankind.

(b) The Congress declares that the general welfare and security of the United States require that adequate provision be made for aeronautical and space activities. The Congress further declares that such activities shall be the responsibility of, and shall be directed by, a civilian agency exercising control over aeronautical and space activities sponsored by the United States, except that activities peculiar to or primarily associated with the development of weapons systems, military operations, or the defense of the United States (including the research and development necessary to make effective provision for the defense of the United States) shall be the responsibility of, and shall be directed by, the Department of Defense; and that determination as to which such agency has responsibility for and direction of any such activity shall be made by the President in conformity with section 201 (e).

(c) The aeronautical and space activities of the United States shall be conducted so as to contribute materially to one or more of the following objectives:

(1) The expansion of human knowledge of phenomena in the atmosphere and space;

(2) The improvement of the usefulness, performance, speed, safety, and efficiency of aeronautical and space vehicles;

(3) The development and operation of vehicles capable of carrying instruments, equipment, supplies, and living organisms through space;

(4) The establishment of long-range studies of the potential benefits to be gained from, the opportunities for, and the problems involved in the utilization of aeronautical and space activities for peaceful and scientific purposes;

(5) The preservation of the role of the United States as a leader in aeronautical and space science and technology and in the application thereof to the conduct of peaceful activities within and outside the atmosphere;

(6) The making available to agencies directly concerned with national defense of discoveries that have military value or significance, and the furnishing by such agencies, to the civilian agency established to direct and control nonmilitary aeronautical and space activities, of information as to discoveries which have value or significance to that agency;

H. R. 12575—2

(7) Cooperation by the United States with other nations and groups of nations in work done pursuant to this Act and in the peaceful application of the results thereof; and

(8) The most effective utilization of the scientific and engineering resources of the United States, with close cooperation among all interested agencies of the United States in order to avoid unnecessary duplication of effort, facilities, and equipment.

(d) It is the purpose of this Act to carry out and effectuate the policies declared in subsections (a), (b), and (c).

DEFINITIONS

SEC. 103. As used in this Act—

(1) the term "aeronautical and space activities" means (A) research into, and the solution of, problems of flight within and outside the earth's atmosphere, (B) the development, construction, testing, and operation for research purposes of aeronautical and space vehicles, and (C) such other activities as may be required for the exploration of space; and

(2) the term "aeronautical and space vehicles" means aircraft, missiles, satellites, and other space vehicles, manned and unmanned, together with related equipment, devices, components, and parts.

TITLE II—COORDINATION OF AERONAUTICAL AND SPACE ACTIVITIES

NATIONAL AERONAUTICS AND SPACE COUNCIL

SEC. 201. (a) There is hereby established the National Aeronautics and Space Council (hereinafter called the "Council") which shall be composed of—

(1) the President (who shall preside over meetings of the Council);

(2) the Secretary of State;

(3) the Secretary of Defense;

(4) the Administrator of the National Aeronautics and Space Administration;

(5) the Chairman of the Atomic Energy Commission;

(6) not more than one additional member appointed by the President from the departments and agencies of the Federal Government; and

(7) not more than three other members appointed by the President, solely on the basis of established records of distinguished achievement, from among individuals in private life who are eminent in science, engineering, technology, education, administration, or public affairs.

(b) Each member of the Council from a department or agency of the Federal Government may designate another officer of his department or agency to serve on the Council as his alternate in his unavoidable absence.

(c) Each member of the Council appointed or designated under paragraphs (6) and (7) of subsection (a), and each alternate member designated under subsection (b), shall be appointed or designated to serve as such by and with the advice and consent of the Senate, unless at the time of such appointment or designation he holds an office in the Federal Government to which he was appointed by and with the advice and consent of the Senate.

H. R. 12575—3

(d) It shall be the function of the Council to advise the President with respect to the performance of the duties prescribed in subsection (e) of this section.

(e) In conformity with the provisions of section 102 of this Act, it shall be the duty of the President to—

(1) survey all significant aeronautical and space activities, including the policies, plans, programs, and accomplishments of all agencies of the United States engaged in such activities;

(2) develop a comprehensive program of aeronautical and space activities to be conducted by agencies of the United States;

(3) designate and fix responsibility for the direction of major aeronautical and space activities;

(4) provide for effective cooperation between the National Aeronautics and Space Administration and the Department of Defense in all such activities, and specify which of such activities may be carried on concurrently by both such agencies notwithstanding the assignment of primary responsibility therefor to one or the other of such agencies; and

(5) resolve differences arising among departments and agencies of the United States with respect to aeronautical and space activities under this Act, including differences as to whether a particular project is an aeronautical and space activity.

(f) The Council may employ a staff to be headed by a civilian executive secretary who shall be appointed by the President by and with the advice and consent of the Senate and shall receive compensation at the rate of $20,000 a year. The executive secretary, subject to the direction of the Council, is authorized to appoint and fix the compensation of such personnel, including not more than three persons who may be appointed without regard to the civil service laws or the Classification Act of 1949 and compensated at the rate of not more than $19,000 a year, as may be necessary to perform such duties as may be prescribed by the Council in connection with the performance of its functions. Each appointment under this subsection shall be subject to the same security requirements as those established for personnel of the National Aeronautics and Space Administration appointed under section 203 (b) (2) of this Act.

(g) Members of the Council appointed from private life under subsection (a) (7) may be compensated at a rate not to exceed $100 per diem, and may be paid travel expenses and per diem in lieu of subsistence in accordance with the provisions of section 5 of the Administrative Expenses Act of 1946 (5 U. S. C. 73b-2) relating to persons serving without compensation.

NATIONAL AERONAUTICS AND SPACE ADMINISTRATION

Sec. 202. (a) There is hereby established the National Aeronautics and Space Administration (hereinafter called the "Administration"). The Administration shall be headed by an Administrator, who shall be appointed from civilian life by the President by and with the advice and consent of the Senate, and shall receive compensation at the rate of $22,500 per annum. Under the supervision and direction of the President, the Administrator shall be responsible for the exercise of all powers and the discharge of all duties of the Administration, and shall have authority and control over all personnel and activities thereof.

(b) There shall be in the Administration a Deputy Administrator, who shall be appointed from civilian life by the President by and with the advice and consent of the Senate, shall receive compensation at the rate of $21,500 per annum, and shall perform such duties and exercise

H. R. 12575—4

such powers as the Administrator may prescribe. The Deputy Administrator shall act for, and exercise the powers of, the Administrator during his absence or disability.

(c) The Administrator and the Deputy Administrator shall not engage in any other business, vocation, or employment while serving as such.

FUNCTIONS OF THE ADMINISTRATION

SEC. 203. (a) The Administration, in order to carry out the purpose of this Act, shall—

(1) plan, direct, and conduct aeronautical and space activities;

(2) arrange for participation by the scientific community in planning scientific measurements and observations to be made through use of aeronautical and space vehicles, and conduct or arrange for the conduct of such measurements and observations; and

(3) provide for the widest practicable and appropriate dissemination of information concerning its activities and the results thereof.

(b) In the performance of its functions the Administration is authorized—

(1) to make, promulgate, issue, rescind, and amend rules and regulations governing the manner of its operations and the exercise of the powers vested in it by law;

(2) to appoint and fix the compensation of such officers and employees as may be necessary to carry out such functions. Such officers and employees shall be appointed in accordance with the civil-service laws and their compensation fixed in accordance with the Classification Act of 1949, except that (A) to the extent the Administrator deems such action necessary to the discharge of his responsibilities, he may appoint and fix the compensation (up to a limit of $19,000 a year, or up to a limit of $21,000 a year for a maximum of ten positions) of not more than two hundred and sixty of the scientific, engineering, and administrative personnel of the Administration without regard to such laws, and (B) to the extent the Administrator deems such action necessary to recruit specially qualified scientific and engineering talent, he may establish the entrance grade for scientific and engineering personnel without previous service in the Federal Government at a level up to two grades higher than the grade provided for such personnel under the General Schedule established by the Classification Act of 1949, and fix their compensation accordingly;

(3) to acquire (by purchase, lease, condemnation, or otherwise), construct, improve, repair, operate, and maintain laboratories, research and testing sites and facilities, aeronautical and space vehicles, quarters and related accommodations for employees and dependents of employees of the Administration, and such other real and personal property (including patents), or any interest therein, as the Administration deems necessary within and outside the continental United States; to lease to others such real and personal property; to sell and otherwise dispose of real and personal property (including patents and rights thereunder) in accordance with the provisions of the Federal Property and Administrative Services Act of 1949, as amended (40 U. S. C. 471 et seq.); and to provide by contract or otherwise for cafeterias and other necessary facilities for the welfare of employees of the Administration at its installations and purchase and maintain equipment therefor;

H. R. 12575—5

(4) to accept unconditional gifts or donations of services, money, or property, real, personal, or mixed, tangible or intangible;

(5) without regard to section 3648 of the Revised Statutes, as amended (31 U. S. C. 529), to enter into and perform such contracts, leases, cooperative agreements, or other transactions as may be necessary in the conduct of its work and on such terms as it may deem appropriate, with any agency or instrumentality of the United States, or with any State, Territory, or possession, or with any political subdivision thereof, or with any person, firm, association, corporation, or educational institution. To the maximum extent practicable and consistent with the accomplishment of the purpose of this Act, such contracts, leases, agreements, and other transactions shall be allocated by the Administrator in a manner which will enable small-business concerns to participate equitably and proportionately in the conduct of the work of the Administration;

(6) to use, with their consent, the services, equipment, personnel, and facilities of Federal and other agencies with or without reimbursement, and on a similar basis to cooperate with other public and private agencies and instrumentalities in the use of services, equipment, and facilities. Each department and agency of the Federal Government shall cooperate fully with the Administration in making its services, equipment, personnel, and facilities available to the Administration, and any such department or agency is authorized, notwithstanding any other provision of law, to transfer to or to receive from the Administration, without reimbursement, aeronautical and space vehicles, and supplies and equipment other than administrative supplies or equipment;

(7) to appoint such advisory committees as may be appropriate for purposes of consultation and advice to the Administration in the performance of its functions;

(8) to establish within the Administration such offices and procedures as may be appropriate to provide for the greatest possible coordination of its activities under this Act with related scientific and other activities being carried on by other public and private agencies and organizations;

(9) to obtain services as authorized by section 15 of the Act of August 2, 1946 (5 U. S. C. 55a), at rates not to exceed $100 per diem for individuals;

(10) when determined by the Administrator to be necessary, and subject to such security investigations as he may determine to be appropriate, to employ aliens without regard to statutory provisions prohibiting payment of compensation to aliens;

(11) to employ retired commissioned officers of the armed forces of the United States and compensate them at the rate established for the positions occupied by them within the Administration, subject only to the limitations in pay set forth in section 212 of the Act of June 30, 1932, as amended (5 U. S. C. 59a);

(12) with the approval of the President, to enter into cooperative agreements under which members of the Army, Navy, Air Force, and Marine Corps may be detailed by the appropriate Secretary for services in the performance of functions under this Act to the same extent as that to which they might be lawfully assigned in the Department of Defense; and

(13) (A) to consider, ascertain, adjust, determine, settle, and pay, on behalf of the United States, in full satisfaction thereof, any claim for $5,000 or less against the United States for bodily injury, death, or damage to or loss of real or personal property

H. R. 12575—6

resulting from the conduct of the Administration's functions as specified in subsection (a) of this section, where such claim is presented to the Administration in writing within two years after the accident or incident out of which the claim arises; and

(B) if the Administration considers that a claim in excess of $5,000 is meritorious and would otherwise be covered by this paragraph, to report the facts and circumstances thereof to the Congress for its consideration.

CIVILIAN-MILITARY LIAISON COMMITTEE

SEC. 204. (a) There shall be a Civilian-Military Liaison Committee consisting of—

(1) a Chairman, who shall be the head thereof and who shall be appointed by the President, shall serve at the pleasure of the President, and shall receive compensation (in the manner provided in subsection (d)) at the rate of $20,000 per annum;

(2) one or more representatives from the Department of Defense, and one or more representatives from each of the Departments of the Army, Navy, and Air Force, to be assigned by the Secretary of Defense to serve on the Committee without additional compensation; and

(3) representatives from the Administration, to be assigned by the Administrator to serve on the Committee without additional compensation, equal in number to the number of representatives assigned to serve on the Committee under paragraph (2).

(b) The Administration and the Department of Defense, through the Liaison Committee, shall advise and consult with each other on all matters within their respective jurisdictions relating to aeronautical and space activities and shall keep each other fully and currently informed with respect to such activities.

(c) If the Secretary of Defense concludes that any request, action, proposed action, or failure to act on the part of the Administrator is adverse to the responsibilities of the Department of Defense, or the Administrator concludes that any request, action, proposed action, or failure to act on the part of the Department of Defense is adverse to the responsibilities of the Administration, and the Administrator and the Secretary of Defense are unable to reach an agreement with respect thereto, either the Administrator or the Secretary of Defense may refer the matter to the President for his decision (which shall be final) as provided in section 201 (e).

(d) Notwithstanding the provisions of any other law, any active or retired officer of the Army, Navy, or Air Force may serve as Chairman of the Liaison Committee without prejudice to his active or retired status as such officer. The compensation received by any such officer for his service as Chairman of the Liaison Committee shall be equal to the amount (if any) by which the compensation fixed by subsection (a) (1) for such Chairman exceeds his pay and allowances (including special and incentive pays) as an active officer, or his retired pay.

INTERNATIONAL COOPERATION

SEC. 205. The Administration, under the foreign policy guidance of the President, may engage in a program of international cooperation in work done pursuant to this Act, and in the peaceful application of the results thereof, pursuant to agreements made by the President with the advice and consent of the Senate.

H. R. 12575—7

REPORTS TO THE CONGRESS

SEC. 206. (a) The Administration shall submit to the President for transmittal to the Congress, semiannually and at such other times as it deems desirable, a report of its activities and accomplishments.

(b) The President shall transmit to the Congress in January of each year a report, which shall include (1) a comprehensive description of the programed activities and the accomplishments of all agencies of the United States in the field of aeronautics and space activities during the preceding calendar year, and (2) an evaluation of such activities and accomplishments in terms of the attainment of, or the failure to attain, the objectives described in section 102 (c) of this Act.

(c) Any report made under this section shall contain such recommendations for additional legislation as the Administrator or the President may consider necessary or desirable for the attainment of the objectives described in section 102 (c) of this Act.

(d) No information which has been classified for reasons of national security shall be included in any report made under this section, unless such information has been declassified by, or pursuant to authorization given by, the President.

TITLE III—MISCELLANEOUS

NATIONAL ADVISORY COMMITTEE FOR AERONAUTICS

SEC. 301. (a) The National Advisory Committee for Aeronautics, on the effective date of this section, shall cease to exist. On such date all functions, powers, duties, and obligations, and all real and personal property, personnel (other than members of the Committee), funds, and records of that organization, shall be transferred to the Administration.

(b) Section 2302 of title 10 of the United States Code is amended by striking out "or the Executive Secretary of the National Advisory Committee for Aeronautics." and inserting in lieu thereof "or the Administrator of the National Aeronautics and Space Administration."; and section 2303 of such title 10 is amended by striking out "The National Advisory Committee for Aeronautics." and inserting in lieu thereof "The National Aeronautics and Space Administration."

(c) The first section of the Act of August 26, 1950 (5 U. S. C. 22-1), is amended by striking out "the Director, National Advisory Committee for Aeronautics" and inserting in lieu thereof "the Administrator of the National Aeronautics and Space Administration", and by striking out "or National Advisory Committee for Aeronautics" and inserting in lieu thereof "or National Aeronautics and Space Administration".

(d) The Unitary Wind Tunnel Plan Act of 1949 (50 U. S. C. 511–515) is amended (1) by striking out "The National Advisory Committee for Aeronautics (hereinafter referred to as the 'Committee')" and inserting in lieu thereof "The Administrator of the National Aeronautics and Space Administration (hereinafter referred to as the 'Administrator')"; (2) by striking out "Committee" or "Committee's" wherever they appear and inserting in lieu thereof "Administrator" and "Administrator's", respectively; and (3) by striking out "its" wherever it appears and inserting in lieu thereof "his".

(e) This section shall take effect ninety days after the date of the enactment of this Act, or on any earlier date on which the Administrator shall determine, and announce by proclamation published in the Federal Register, that the Administration has been organized and is prepared to discharge the duties and exercise the powers conferred upon it by this Act.

H. R. 12575—8

TRANSFER OF RELATED FUNCTIONS

SEC. 302. (a) Subject to the provisions of this section, the President, for a period of four years after the date of enactment of this Act, may transfer to the Administration any functions (including powers, duties, activities, facilities, and parts of functions) of any other department or agency of the United States, or of any officer or organizational entity thereof, which relate primarily to the functions, powers, and duties of the Administration as prescribed by section 203 of this Act. In connection with any such transfer, the President may, under this section or other applicable authority, provide for appropriate transfers of records, property, civilian personnel, and funds.

(b) Whenever any such transfer is made before January 1, 1959, the President shall transmit to the Speaker of the House of Representatives and the President pro tempore of the Senate a full and complete report concerning the nature and effect of such transfer.

(c) After December 31, 1958, no transfer shall be made under this section until (1) a full and complete report concerning the nature and effect of such proposed transfer has been transmitted by the President to the Congress, and (2) the first period of sixty calendar days of regular session of the Congress following the date of receipt of such report by the Congress has expired without the adoption by the Congress of a concurrent resolution stating that the Congress does not favor such transfer.

ACCESS TO INFORMATION

SEC. 303. Information obtained or developed by the Administrator in the performance of his functions under this Act shall be made available for public inspection, except (A) information authorized or required by Federal statute to be withheld, and (B) information classified to protect the national security: *Provided*, That nothing in this Act shall authorize the withholding of information by the Administrator from the duly authorized committees of the Congress.

SECURITY

SEC. 304. (a) The Administrator shall establish such security requirements, restrictions, and safeguards as he deems necessary in the interest of the national security. The Administrator may arrange with the Civil Service Commission for the conduct of such security or other personnel investigations of the Administration's officers, employees, and consultants, and its contractors and subcontractors and their officers and employees, actual or prospective, as he deems appropriate; and if any such investigation develops any data reflecting that the individual who is the subject thereof is of questionable loyalty the matter shall be referred to the Federal Bureau of Investigation for the conduct of a full field investigation, the results of which shall be furnished to the Administrator.

(b) The Atomic Energy Commission may authorize any of its employees, or employees of any contractor, prospective contractor, licensee, or prospective licensee of the Atomic Energy Commission or any other person authorized to have access to Restricted Data by the Atomic Energy Commission under subsection 145 b. of the Atomic Energy Act of 1954 (42 U. S. C. 2165 (b)), to permit any member, officer, or employee of the Council, or the Administrator, or any officer, employee, member of an advisory committee, contractor, subcontractor, or officer or employee of a contractor or subcontractor of the Administration, to have access to Restricted Data relating to aeronautical and space activities which is required in the performance of his duties and so certified by the Council or the Administrator, as the case may be,

H. R. 12575—9

but only if (1) the Council or Administrator or designee thereof has determined, in accordance with the established personnel security procedures and standards of the Council or Administration, that permitting such individual to have access to such Restricted Data will not endanger the common defense and security, and (2) the Council or Administrator or designee thereof finds that the established personnel and other security procedures and standards of the Council or Administration are adequate and in reasonable conformity to the standards established by the Atomic Energy Commission under section 145 of the Atomic Energy Act of 1954 (42 U. S. C. 2165). Any individual granted access to such Restricted Data pursuant to this subsection may exchange such Data with any individual who (A) is an officer or employee of the Department of Defense, or any department or agency thereof, or a member of the armed forces, or a contractor or subcontractor of any such department, agency, or armed force, or an officer or employee of any such contractor or subcontractor, and (B) has been authorized to have access to Restricted Data under the provisions of section 143 of the Atomic Energy Act of 1954 (42 U. S. C. 2163).

(c) Chapter 37 of title 18 of the United States Code (entitled Espionage and Censorship) is amended by—

(1) adding at the end thereof the following new section:

"§ 790. Violation of regulations of National Aeronautics and Space Administration

"Whoever willfully shall violate, attempt to violate, or conspire to violate any regulation or order promulgated by the Administrator of the National Aeronautics and Space Administration for the protection or security of any laboratory, station, base or other facility, or part thereof, or any aircraft, missile, spacecraft, or similar vehicle, or part thereof, or other property or equipment in the custody of the Administration, or any real or personal property or equipment in the custody of any contractor under any contract with the Administration or any subcontractor of any such contractor, shall be fined not more than $5,000, or imprisoned not more than one year, or both."

(2) adding at the end of the sectional analysis thereof the following new item:

"790. Violation of regulations of National Aeronautics and Space Administration."

(d) Section 1114 of title 18 of the United States Code is amended by inserting immediately before "while engaged in the performance of his official duties" the following: "or any officer or employee of the National Aeronautics and Space Administration directed to guard and protect property of the United States under the administration and control of the National Aeronautics and Space Administration,".

(e) The Administrator may direct such of the officers and employees of the Administration as he deems necessary in the public interest to carry firearms while in the conduct of their official duties. The Administrator may also authorize such of those employees of the contractors and subcontractors of the Administration engaged in the protection of property owned by the United States and located at facilities owned by or contracted to the United States as he deems necessary in the public interest, to carry firearms while in the conduct of their official duties.

PROPERTY RIGHTS IN INVENTIONS

SEC. 305. (a) Whenever any invention is made in the performance of any work under any contract of the Administration, and the Administrator determines that—

(1) the person who made the invention was employed or assigned to perform research, development, or exploration work and the invention is related to the work he was employed or

H. R. 12575—10

assigned to perform, or that it was within the scope of his employment duties, whether or not it was made during working hours, or with a contribution by the Government of the use of Government facilities, equipment, materials, allocated funds, information proprietary to the Government, or services of Government employees during working hours; or

(2) the person who made the invention was not employed or assigned to perform research, development, or exploration work, but the invention is nevertheless related to the contract, or to the work or duties he was employed or assigned to perform, and was made during working hours, or with a contribution from the Government of the sort referred to in clause (1),

such invention shall be the exclusive property of the United States, and if such invention is patentable a patent therefor shall be issued to the United States upon application made by the Administrator, unless the Administrator waives all or any part of the rights of the United States to such invention in conformity with the provisions of subsection (f) of this section.

(b) Each contract entered into by the Administrator with any party for the performance of any work shall contain effective provisions under which such party shall furnish promptly to the Administrator a written report containing full and complete technical information concerning any invention, discovery, improvement, or innovation which may be made in the performance of any such work.

(c) No patent may be issued to any applicant other than the Administrator for any invention which appears to the Commissioner of Patents to have significant utility in the conduct of aeronautical and space activities unless the applicant files with the Commissioner, with the application or within thirty days after request therefor by the Commissioner, a written statement executed under oath setting forth the full facts concerning the circumstances under which such invention was made and stating the relationship (if any) of such invention to the performance of any work under any contract of the Administration. Copies of each such statement and the application to which it relates shall be transmitted forthwith by the Commissioner to the Administrator.

(d) Upon any application as to which any such statement has been transmitted to the Administrator, the Commissioner may, if the invention is patentable, issue a patent to the applicant unless the Administrator, within ninety days after receipt of such application and statement, requests that such patent be issued to him on behalf of the United States. If, within such time, the Administrator files such a request with the Commissioner, the Commissioner shall transmit notice thereof to the applicant, and shall issue such patent to the Administrator unless the applicant within thirty days after receipt of such notice requests a hearing before a Board of Patent Interferences on the question whether the Administrator is entitled under this section to receive such patent. The Board may hear and determine, in accordance with rules and procedures established for interference cases, the question so presented, and its determination shall be subject to appeal by the applicant or by the Administrator to the Court of Customs and Patent Appeals in accordance with procedures governing appeals from decisions of the Board of Patent Interferences in other proceedings.

(e) Whenever any patent has been issued to any applicant in conformity with subsection (d), and the Administrator thereafter has reason to believe that the statement filed by the applicant in connection therewith contained any false representation of any material fact, the Administrator within five years after the date of issuance of such patent may file with the Commissioner a request for the trans-

H. R. 12575—11

fer to the Administrator of title to such patent on the records of the Commissioner. Notice of any such request shall be transmitted by the Commissioner to the owner of record of such patent, and title to such patent shall be so transferred to the Administrator unless within thirty days after receipt of such notice such owner of record requests a hearing before a Board of Patent Interferences on the question whether any such false representation was contained in such statement. Such question shall be heard and determined, and determination thereof shall be subject to review, in the manner prescribed by subsection (d) for questions arising thereunder. No request made by the Administrator under this subsection for the transfer of title to any patent, and no prosecution for the violation of any criminal statute, shall be barred by any failure of the Administrator to make a request under subsection (d) for the issuance of such patent to him, or by any notice previously given by the Administrator stating that he had no objection to the issuance of such patent to the applicant therefor.

(f) Under such regulations in conformity with this subsection as the Administrator shall prescribe, he may waive all or any part of the rights of the United States under this section with respect to any invention or class of inventions made or which may be made by any person or class of persons in the performance of any work required by any contract of the Administration if the Administrator determines that the interests of the United States will be served thereby. Any such waiver may be made upon such terms and under such conditions as the Administrator shall determine to be required for the protection of the interests of the United States. Each such waiver made with respect to any invention shall be subject to the reservation by the Administrator of an irrevocable, nonexclusive, nontransferrable, royalty-free license for the practice of such invention throughout the world by or on behalf of the United States or any foreign government pursuant to any treaty or agreement with the United States. Each proposal for any waiver under this subsection shall be referred to an Inventions and Contributions Board which shall be established by the Administrator within the Administration. Such Board shall accord to each interested party an opportunity for hearing, and shall transmit to the Administrator its findings of fact with respect to such proposal and its recommendations for action to be taken with respect thereto.

(g) The Administrator shall determine, and promulgate regulations specifying, the terms and conditions upon which licenses will be granted by the Administration for the practice by any person (other than an agency of the United States) of any invention for which the Administrator holds a patent on behalf of the United States.

(h) The Administrator is authorized to take all suitable and necessary steps to protect any invention or discovery to which he has title, and to require that contractors or persons who retain title to inventions or discoveries under this section protect the inventions or discoveries to which the Administration has or may acquire a license of use.

(i) The Administration shall be considered a defense agency of the United States for the purpose of chapter 17 of title 35 of the United States Code.

(j) As used in this section—

(1) the term "person" means any individual, partnership, corporation, association, institution, or other entity;

(2) the term "contract" means any actual or proposed contract, agreement, understanding, or other arrangement, and includes any assignment, substitution of parties, or subcontract executed or entered into thereunder; and

H. R. 12575—12

(3) the term "made", when used in relation to any invention, means the conception or first actual reduction to practice of such invention.

CONTRIBUTIONS AWARDS

SEC. 306. (a) Subject to the provisions of this section, the Administrator is authorized, upon his own initiative or upon application of any person, to make a monetary award, in such amount and upon such terms as he shall determine to be warranted, to any person (as defined by section 305) for any scientific or technical contribution to the Administration which is determined by the Administrator to have significant value in the conduct of aeronautical and space activities. Each application made for any such award shall be referred to the Inventions and Contributions Board established under section 305 of this Act. Such Board shall accord to each such applicant an opportunity for hearing upon such application, and shall transmit to the Administrator its recommendation as to the terms of the award, if any, to be made to such applicant for such contribution. In determining the terms and conditions of any award the Administrator shall take into account—

(1) the value of the contribution to the United States;
(2) the aggregate amount of any sums which have been expended by the applicant for the development of such contribution;
(3) the amount of any compensation (other than salary received for services rendered as an officer or employee of the Government) previously received by the applicant for or on account of the use of such contribution by the United States; and
(4) such other factors as the Administrator shall determine to be material.

(b) If more than one applicant under subsection (a) claims an interest in the same contribution, the Administrator shall ascertain and determine the respective interests of such applicants, and shall apportion any award to be made with respect to such contribution among such applicants in such proportions as he shall determine to be equitable. No award may be made under subsection (a) with respect to any contribution—

(1) unless the applicant surrenders, by such means as the Administrator shall determine to be effective, all claims which such applicant may have to receive any compensation (other than the award made under this section) for the use of such contribution or any element thereof at any time by or on behalf of the United States, or by or on behalf of any foreign government pursuant to any treaty or agreement with the United States, within the United States or at any other place;
(2) in any amount exceeding $100,000, unless the Administrator has transmitted to the appropriate committees of the Congress a full and complete report concerning the amount and terms of, and the basis for, such proposed award, and thirty calendar days of regular session of the Congress have expired after receipt of such report by such committees.

H. R. 12575—12

(3) the term "made", when used in relation to any invention, means the conception or first actual reduction to practice of such invention.

CONTRIBUTIONS AWARDS

SEC. 306. (a) Subject to the provisions of this section, the Administrator is authorized, upon his own initiative or upon application of any person, to make a monetary award, in such amount and upon such terms as he shall determine to be warranted, to any person (as defined by section 305) for any scientific or technical contribution to the Administration which is determined by the Administrator to have significant value in the conduct of aeronautical and space activities. Each application made for any such award shall be referred to the Inventions and Contributions Board established under section 305 of this Act. Such Board shall accord to each such applicant an opportunity for hearing upon such application, and shall transmit to the Administrator its recommendation as to the terms of the award, if any, to be made to such applicant for such contribution. In determining the terms and conditions of any award the Administrator shall take into account—

(1) the value of the contribution to the United States;

(2) the aggregate amount of any sums which have been expended by the applicant for the development of such contribution;

(3) the amount of any compensation (other than salary received for services rendered as an officer or employee of the Government) previously received by the applicant for or on account of the use of such contribution by the United States; and

(4) such other factors as the Administrator shall determine to be material.

(b) If more than one applicant under subsection (a) claims an interest in the same contribution, the Administrator shall ascertain and determine the respective interests of such applicants, and shall apportion any award to be made with respect to such contribution among such applicants in such proportions as he shall determine to be equitable. No award may be made under subsection (a) with respect to any contribution—

(1) unless the applicant surrenders, by such means as the Administrator shall determine to be effective, all claims which such applicant may have to receive any compensation (other than the award made under this section) for the use of such contribution or any element thereof at any time by or on behalf of the United States, or by or on behalf of any foreign government pursuant to any treaty or agreement with the United States, within the United States or at any other place;

(2) in any amount exceeding $100,000, unless the Administrator has transmitted to the appropriate committees of the Congress a full and complete report concerning the amount and terms of, and the basis for, such proposed award, and thirty calendar days of regular session of the Congress have expired after receipt of such report by such committees.

H. R. 12575—13

APPROPRIATIONS

SEC. 307. (a) There are hereby authorized to be appropriated such sums as may be necessary to carry out this Act, except that nothing in this Act shall authorize the appropriation of any amount for (1) the acquisition or condemnation of any real property, or (2) any other item of a capital nature (such as plant or facility acquisition, construction, or expansion) which exceeds $250,000. Sums appropriated pursuant to this subsection for the construction of facilities, or for research and development activities, shall remain available until expended.

(b) Any funds appropriated for the construction of facilities may be used for emergency repairs of existing facilities when such existing facilities are made inoperative by major breakdown, accident, or other circumstances and such repairs are deemed by the Administrator to be of greater urgency than the construction of new facilities.

Speaker of the House of Representatives.

Vice President of the United States and President of the Senate.

APPROVED
JUL 29 1958

NASA's Origins and the Dawn of the Space Age

Document 9

Title: Special Committee on Space Technology, "Recommendations to the NASA Regarding a National Civil Space Program," October 28, 1958.

Source: NASA Historical Reference Collection, History Office, NASA Headquarters, Washington, D.C.

By the end of 1957, the NACA was heavily involved in space-related research, which constituted 40 to 50 percent of its total effort. Sensing that the NACA might be the obvious choice for taking the lead in the American space effort after Sputnik, on January 12, 1958, General James Doolittle, the NACA's chair, created a Special Committee on Space Technology. While NACA Director Hugh Dryden addressed the institutional issues involved in transforming the NACA into NASA, the Special Committee on Space Technology was charged with addressing specific areas of space technology deserving early attention. NASA was formally established on October 1, 1958, and the committee issued its final report at the end of that month. The following document reprints the recommendations to NASA on a national civil space program offered by the committee on October 28, 1958.

RECOMMENDATIONS

To the NASA Regarding

A NATIONAL CIVIL SPACE PROGRAM

by the

Special Committee on Space Technology

October 28, 1958

INDEX

Summary. 1

Introduction 2

Objectives 3

Basic Scientific Research. 5
   Space Research
   Upper Atmosphere Research
   Ground-Based Supporting Research

Research Techniques and Equipment Development 7
   Vehicle Instrumentation
   Ground Simulation
   Flight Testing Techniques

Ground Facilities. 9
   Range Capabilities and Requirements
   Ground-Based Instrumentation Systems
   Real-Time Communication
   Recovery
   Space Surveillance

Flight Program 13
   Re-entry Vehicles
   Propulsion
   Vehicles for Early Experiments

Conclusion. 15

SUMMARY

The major objectives of a civil space research program are scientific research in the physical and life sciences, advancement of space flight technology, development of manned space flight capability, and exploitation of space flight for human benefit. Inherent in the achievement of these objectives is the development and unification of new scientific concepts of unforeseeably broad import.

Space Research - Instruments mounted in space vehicles can observe and measure "geophysical" and environmental phenomena in the solar system, the results of cosmic processes in outer space, and atmospheric phenomena, as well as the influence of the space environment on materials and living organisms. A vigorous, coordinated attack upon the problems of maintaining the performance capabilities of man in the space environment is prerequisite to sophisticated space exploration.

Development - Flight vehicles and simulators should be used for space research and also for developmental testing and evaluation aimed at improved space flight and observational capabilities. Major developmental recommendations include sustained support of a comprehensive instrumentation development program, establishment of versatile dynamic flight simulators, and provision of a coordinated series of vehicles for testing components and sub-systems.

Ground Facilities - Properly diversified space flight operations are impossible without adequate ground facilities. To this end serious study aimed toward providing an equatorial launching capability is recommended. A complete ground instrumentation system consisting of computing centers, communication network, and facilities for tracking and control of and communication (including telemetry) with space vehicles is required. At least part of the system must be capable of real time computation and communication, primarily for manned flights and payload recovery. Development of a competent satellite communications relay system would be most valuable in this regard, and it is recommended that NASA take the lead in determining the specifications of such a system. A coordinated national attack upon the problems of recovery is recommended.

Flight Program - The first recovery vehicles will probably be ballistic, but the control and safety advantages of lifting re-entry vehicles warrant their development.

A million-pound-plus booster can be achieved about three years sooner by clustering existing engines than by developing a new single-barrel engine, but the cluster would not have the growth potential of the larger engine. Further growth potential requires the development of the single-barrel engine. Both developments are needed.

Strong research effort on novel propulsion systems for vacuum operations is urged, and development of high-energy-propellant systems for upper stages should receive full support.

Three generations of space vehicles are immediately available. The first is based on Vanguard-Jupiter C, the second on IRBM boosters, and the third on ICBM boosters. The performance capabilities of various combinations of existing boosters and upper stages should be evaluated, and intensive development concentrated on those promising greatest usefulness in different general categories of payload.

INTRODUCTION

Scientifically, we are at the beginning of a new era. More than two centuries between Newton and Einstein were occupied by the observations, experiments and thought that produced the background necessary for modern science. New scientific knowledge indicates that we are already working in a similar period preceding another long step forward in scientific theory. The information obtained from direct observation, in space, of environment and of cosmological processes will probably be essential to, and will certainly assist in, the formulation of new unifying theories. We can no more predict the results of this work than Galileo could have predicted the industrial revolution that resulted from Newtonian mechanics.

Direct observation of the nature and effects of the space environment are necessarily paced by the development of space flight capabilities. This report presents suggestions regarding research policies and procedures that should aid in the establishment and improvement of capabilities for space flight and space research.

In preparing this report, the Special Committee on Space Technology has been assisted by the Technical Committees of the NACA and the ad hoc Working Groups of the Special Committee. The membership of the Working Groups is listed in an appendix to this report.

The reports of the Working Groups are primarily program-oriented, and while they are not referenced specifically, they have furnished the basis for the preparation of this report. These will be presented to the NASA as separate Working Group reports, independent of this report.

3

OBJECTIVES

A national civil space research program to explore, study, and conquer the newly accessible realm beyond the atmosphere will have the following general objectives:

1. Scientific research and exploration in the physical and the life sciences.

Submerged as he always has been beneath the "dirty window" of the atmosphere, man has necessarily inferred the nature of the physical universe from local observations and glimpses of what lies beyond his essentially two-dimensional earth-bound habitat. Little of the radiation and few of the solid particles from outer space reach the earth's surface, yet practically all aspects of man's earthly environment are determined ultimately by extraterrestrial factors. The radiation that does reach the surface is so distorted by passage through the atmosphere that only incomplete observations can be made on the nature of other celestial bodies and the contents of interstellar space.

With the information derived from experiments and direct observations in the actual space environment, man will achieve a better understanding of the universe and of natural phenomena and life on the earth.

An excellent start toward determination of the near-space environment has already been made in connection with the IGY, and the pattern of inter-national cooperation that has developed with this program indicates that mutual understanding and respect among the nations of the earth may be generated by concerted attack upon scientific problems. Inasmuch as national scientific excellence is, to a great extent, now evaluated by the peoples of the earth in terms of success in the exploration of space, it behooves the United States to achieve and maintain an unselfish leadership in this field.

2. Advancement of the technology of space flight.

Propulsion systems have been developed having the demonstrated capability of putting small instrumented packages into orbit about the earth. However, the reliability of the total vehicle and control system needs improvement in order to conduct much of the desired space program. Larger power plants, and new higher-energy fuels and the equipment to produce them must be developed. If orbits about the earth are to be expanded into practical interplanetary trajectories, new propulsion systems having very low fuel consumption and modest thrust will be required in order that the trajectory can be controlled to perform the mission.

A good start has been made on the development of instrumentation for observing the environment in space. Instrumentation for controlling and navigating the vehicle and for communicating with the earth will require extensive development. Because of the severe weight restrictions, all instrumentation must be severely miniaturized. Ground-based communication systems must be expanded to provide for the control of and communication with vehicles on lunar or planetary missions, and for properly controlled re-entry and recovery.

Novel structural problems are posed by space vehicles. Heavy loads of steady acceleration, shock and vibration occur during boost, while weightlessness during unpowered space flight makes possible the use of unconventional mechanical design principles. For vehicles which must re-enter the earth's atmosphere, problems of structural integrity under high re-entry heating rates, large thermal gradients, and thermal shock are very important. All of these requirements must be met with an absolute minimum of structural weight.

Extensive human engineering developments are required in order for manned space flight to be successful. Because of the rigorous but largely unknown space environment, these developments will depend critically upon the information obtained in the early probing flights.

A successful National Space Program, therefore, requires continuing improvement and development in the pertinent fields of technology.

3. Manned space flight.

Instruments for the collection and transmission of data on the space environment have been designed and put into orbit about the earth. However, man has the capability of correlating unlikely events and unexpected observations, a capacity for overall evaluation of situations, and the background knowledge and experience to apply judgment that cannot be provided by instruments; and in many other ways the intellectual functions of man are a necessary complement to the observing and recording functions of complicated instrument systems. Furthermore, man is capable of voice communication for sending detailed descriptions and receiving information whereby the concerted judgement of others may be brought to bear on unforeseen problems that may arise during flight.

Although it is believed that a manned satellite is not necessary for the collection of environmental data in the vicinity of the earth, exploration of the solar system in a sophisticated way will require a human crew.

4. Exploitation of space for human benefit.

The practical exploitation of satellites and space vehicles for civil purposes and for human benefit may be as important as--or even more important than--the immediate military uses of space flight. Perhaps the most important example is the use of satellite vehicles for active or passive communications relay. This could extend what are effectively line-of-sight communication links for thousands of miles between points on the ground, with very great bandwidths and none of the capriciousness now characterizing long-range HF communications.

Many indirect benefits will also be derived from the technological developments that will make space flight practical. The necessarily high technological standards required for space flight will certainly accelerate improvement in transportation, communication and other contributions to human welfare.

The unpredictable long-term benefits of space-accelerated scientific and technological advancement will almost certainly far exceed the foreseeable benefits.

Aside from the intentional omission of military and political objectives, the foregoing objectives appear to be in consonance with those mentioned in "Introduction to Outer Space," by the President's Science Advisory Committee (Killian Committee), and with the objectives stated in the National Aeronautics and Space Act of 1958, which is the enabling lesiglation for the National Aeronautics and Space Administration.

BASIC SCIENTIFIC RESEARCH

Space Research

Geophysical observations from satellites and non-orbiting space probes enable the gravitational and magnetic fields in the vicinity of the earth to be mapped to altitudes limited only by the capabilities of the flight vehicle. The interactions among these fields and the particles and radiations approaching the earth from the sun and outer space can be studied, and related to the composition and behavior of the gaseous envelope of the earth from troposphere to exosphere. Satellite observations of large-scale cloud movements and other atmospheric phenomena can do much to put meteorology on a more sound scientific basis. As propulsion and guidance systems are improved, "geodetic" and "geophysical" studies can be extended to the moon and other planets.

Telescopes and spectroscopes mounted on earth satellites can utilize the complete radiation spectrum from vacuum ultraviolet to radio frequencies to observe the sun, the planets, stars, and interstellar space. Direct measurements of the space environment should include the nature, direction and intensity of electromagnetic and corpuscular radiation, and the nature and distribution of meteorites. The mass density in space can be measured, and large-scale magneto-hydrodynamic phenomena in and beyond the ionosphere can be studied. These observations and direct measurements will offer tremendous improvements in understanding of cosmic processes.

In addition to scientific observations and environmental measurements, satellite experiments will enable evaluation of the effect of the space environment on all types of material and biological specimens and hardware components. Re-entry phenomena can be studied, and here, for the first time, it is possible to investigate the effects of extended periods of weightlessness on instrumentation and living subjects.

Experiments with man and other living organisms, both plant and animal, during extended periods in the space environment may offer new insight into human physiology and psychology and into life processes generally.

Upper Atmosphere Experiments

Upper atmosphere experiments, utilizing both rocket-propelled and balloon-supported vehicles, can, at reasonable cost, give direct information on both the vertical and time-wise variations of various atmospheric parameters and cosmic radiations. Heat-transfer, ablation, vehicle-control dynamics, and pilot-vehicle interactions can be studied under approximately re-entry conditions. Limited-time biological studies and human physiological and psychological studies under almost space conditions, and with limited periods of weightlessness, can also be investigated.

Ground-Based Supporting Research

In addition to direct study of the space environment, much ground-based research must be conducted as a basis for the space flight program. This will include such factors as radiation effects

7

on materials, instruments, and living organisms, and means of radiation protection. Other phsyical phenomena pertinent to space flight and re-entry include radio propagation; the behavior, in a space-type environment, of materials, transducers, power supplies, and so forth, for instrument components; hypersonic gasdynamics, both continuum and noncontinuum; and magnetogasdynamics.

Human factors pertinent to space flight present a real challenge. Those amenable to ground-based study include, among others, acceleration and vibration tolerance and protection, and the influence of new physiological and psychological factors (other than weightlessness) on the performance capabilities of the crew members. A major cooperative effort between the NASA, the Department of Defense, and other groups concerned with aeromedical and space flight problems is necessary.

RESEARCH TECHNIQUES AND EQUIPMENT DEVELOPMENT

Vehicle Instrumentation

Vehicle instrumentation presents formidable development problems because of the conflicting requirements of minimum weight, adequate resistance to the accelerations and vibrations of launching and ability to operate correctly for extended periods of time under the conditions of space flight. For scientific observations, a complete range of instrumentation will be required for observing the external environment and recording or telemetering the data. Other special instrumentation will be required to observe experiments conducted within the vehicle.

Navigation and guidance equipment, and instruments for attitude sensing and control and for communication, are required for operation of the vehicle, particularly on extended flights into space. An integrated display of information on the internal environment and the vehicle operation will be required for manned flights. Improved auxiliary power sources will be needed for all types of vehicle-borne instruments.

It is recommended that the NASA organize and give consistent support to a comprehensive program of instrumentation development, comprising not only instruments useful in the development, flight testing, and operation of space vehicles, but also the instruments needed for a broad program of environmental and other experimental research. Special attention should be paid to the novel design possibilities offered by operation of such instruments in free fall and in vacuo.

8

Ground Simulation of Environment and Operational Problems

The development and testing of a space vehicle, its components and, for a manned vehicle, its crew require ground simulation of the encironment and operating problems that will be encountered. The completeness of the simulation may well determine the success or failure of the mission. this will be a continuously changing problem as new information is obtained on the environment and as the operational ranges and durations increase.

Wind tunnels and jets of various types, ballistic ranges and structural test facilities, can simulate, to a reasonable extent, aerodynamic effects encountered during launching and re-entry. Vacuum chambers with assorted loading devices and radiation sources will be useful for both instrument and structural tests.

The capacity of a human crew to participate in the operation of a space vehicle is still an unknown quantity. As fast as such capabilities are demonstrated they should be utilized to the extent profitable in the operation of the vehicle. Therefore, flight simulators should be designed and built in which the flight dynamics and internal environment of space vehicles can be simulated as closely as possible. Such facilities would be used for pilot evaluation and training and for evaluation of the dynamic characteristics of the vehicle-pilot combination.

Flight Testing Techniques

To aid in the advanced development of space vehicles and sub-systems, and to complement the ground-based simulators, it is recommended that the NASA use reliable high-performance rocket-propelled test vehicles which would be standardized for as many tests as possible. In order to minimize the development cost of such vehicles, they should presumably be based on military developments in the missile field.

Two other techniques are recommended for larger-scale tests and for systems development and testing. One of these is a large, high-altitude, balloon-supported laboratory in which most conditions of space environment could be simulated. This balloon-supported laboratory would not only allow a substantial amount of research on the equipment needed by the space crew and on the effects of space environment on the capsule and its inhabitants, but could also be valuable for basic environmental studies.

9

The other is a nonorbiting rocket-propelled research vehicle capable of carrying at least two men, or an actual man-carrying satellite capsule. This vehicle should be capable of a number of minutes of free coast well above significant atmospheric influences. Such a vehicle could be used for development and final flight-testing of actual space capsules, for study of various recovery techniques, and for development of space flight controls and operational instrumentation. In addition, flight crews could be trained and evaluated under substantially longer periods of weightlessness than are possible within the atmosphere.

With the establishment of artificial earth satellites, space flight has become a reality, albeit on only a very limited scale. For more extended space missions, the long-time effects of the space environment on the vehicle and its contents must be known and designed for. This can best be studied in earth satellite vehicles. Strong technological support should be provided for all phases of vehicular development. Specifically, a substantial fraction of space flight missions should be allocated to such technological projects as components tests, materials tests, engine-restart tests, solar power supply systems, et cetera.

GROUND FACILITIES
for Space Flight Operations

Range Capabilities and Requirements

In view of the plans to expand the NASA Wallops Island facility for technique development and relatively small probe and satellite launchings, and with the Atlantic and the Pacific Missile Ranges capable of substantial further development, there is no present need for another major nonequatorial launching complex. It may be desirable, however, for the NASA to establish permanent field stations at both the Atlantic and Pacific Missile Ranges.

On the other hand, the unique properties of an equatorial orbit lead to a distinct need for an equatorial launching site. These are:

1. Narrow track over the earth's surface.

2. Best departure point for interplanetary operations.

3. Capability for all other orbits.

4. Minimum requirement for ground stations and communication system.

These considerations bring the Committee to the conclusion that the NASA should establish a study, survey and planning group aimed toward early provision of an equatorial launching capability, including necessary logistic support, for the United States. Fixed-base and ship-based launchings should be considered by the group before reaching a final decision.

Ground-Based Instrumentation System

The ground-based instrumentation needs of the civilian space program encompass such things as:

1. Communication with and transmission of commands to vehicles both near the earth and in interplanetary space.

2. Active and passive tracking of space vehicles.

3. Reception of telemetry signals from space.

4. Calculation of real-time search ephemeris data.

5. Calculation of final orbits for scientific analysis.

The instrumentation necessary can thus be listed as:

1. A network of stations suitably located for tracking of and communication with vehicles in interplanetary space. These stations must be tied together with reasonably rapid communication links. The stations will consist of very large antennas, sensitive receiving equipment, and high-power transmitting equipment.

2. A network of radio receiving stations to obtain orbital information from active satellites. These stations may be, in part at least, the same as those in the preceding paragraph.

3. A network of optical stations to make very precise optical observations on some satellites, and a supplementary set of optical observing stations, probably similar to the present Moonwatch teams, for rough orbital data.

4. A set of telemetry receiving stations which will be in part, but not necessarily completely, at the other radio sites.

5. A special network of stations for re-entry experiments.

6. Computing facilities to calculate and publish search ephemeris data.

7. Computing facilities to generate orbital data of sufficient accuracy to satisfy scientific needs.

11

This complete instrumentation network should be coordinated with similar activities of the Department of Defense, but the special requirements of the civilian space program are such as to require the NASA to establish and operate some of the stations. The technical requirements of the space communication channels, telemetry, et cetera should likewise be coordinated with the Department of Defense.

In view of the radio frequency requirements of the space program for communication with space vehicles, it is recommended that NASA take the necessary steps to insure that frequency assignments for this prupose are available.

Overseas stations of the NASA could be operated by local technical groups, universities, et cetera, and this phase of the problem should be actively pursued by NASA, for reasons both of efficient and economical operation and of international cooperation.

It is recommended that the NASA offer to support the continued operation of the present IGY tracking system for an interim period after the expiration of the present IGY support. It is recommended, however, that a study be made of possible radio tracking systems to replace or supplement the present Minitrack stations. It is believed that a permanent radio tracking system should be capable of receiving signals at higher frequencies and from larger numbers of satellites, should probably offer greater angular coverage, and may require a different geographical plan. Special attention needs to be given to the reception of signals of broader bandwidth to take care of future satellites which may have a relatively large quantity of information to transmit back to earth.

Real-Time Communication

Certain projects will require real-time computation of orbits and communication of the data to other ground stations at large earth distances. A capability for communication with the satellite essentially all the time may also be desirable, particularly for manned flights. It appears, however, that such a situation may not be completely feasible, either technically or economically, in the near future, and therefore the communication system which can be provided may prove to be one of the limiting factors in the design of the experiment. Hard wire, which is considered to be the only currently available communication system whose reliability approaches 100 percent, extends only from Hawaii to Italy by commercial cable. All radio systems of substantial range are less reliable, except for line-of-sight operations such as communication satellites might provide. Since many agencies are concerned with this matter, and many important design decisions must be taken to yield the most

12

generally useful satellite communications relay system, NASA should take the initiative in coordinating the various requirements and settling on a preferred system at the earliest possible date. Furthermore, projects requiring real-time communication should formulate a rather complete communications plan early in the project-planning stage.

Recovery

The requirements for recovery of instrumented and manned satellites from orbital flight pose problems involving equipment, communication, and operation which are of very great magnitude. The escape maneuver during both the launch and the recovery phases will require recovery capability over large areas of the Atlantic Ocean, the Pacific Ocean, and possibly the United States Zone of the Interior.

It appears that a coordinated national effort is required to cope with this problem.

It is recommended, therefore, that NASA establish a working group on recovery systems which will summarize the experience obtained to date, will define the problems to be solved, and propose operational techniques and equipment which should be developed.

One possible solution would be for the Atlantic, Pacific, and White Sands Missile Ranges to establish coordinated operational groups for these three areas, making maximum use of existing organization and facilities, for all national space programs requiring recovery techniques.

Space Surveillance Problems

It is not considered necessary for NASA to set up the ground equipment and to maintain current ephemerides of all passive satellites, although, of course, ephemerides will be required for all satellites during the course of their experiments and for all satellites intended for recovery.

It is considered important that some kind of control be applied to limit the life of any satellite radio transmitter to a reasonable duration of experiment, in order to prevent cluttering up useful parts of the radio spectrum. However, no non-military need is anticipated, at this time, for a "vacuum cleaner" to remove from orbit the satellites that have outlived their usefulness.

13

FLIGHT PROGRAM

Re-entry Vehicles

Types of and uses for non-satellite probes and instrumented satellites have already been commented upon. Manned satellites, however, must be capable of safely re-entering the earth's atmosphere and being recovered. As a result of study of a number of suggested satellite vehicles for manned flight, it is concluded that:

1. The ballistic (pure drag) type vehicle can probably be put in operation soonest because:

   a. The booster problem is simplest by virtue of the low weight of this satellite vehicle.

   b. The aerodynamic heating problem is well understood.

   c. The development of the vehicle appears to be straight-forward.

2. The high-drag, high-lift vehicle study should be carried on concurrently because:

   a. The ability to steer during re-entry eases the recovery problem, since it reduces the accuracy required of the retrograde rocket timing and impulse, and allows the vehicle to be flown to or near the ground or sea recovery stations.

   b. The danger of excessive accidental decelerations due to malfunction in either the boost phase or re-entry phase of flight is greatly diminished.

3. The low-drag, high-lift vehicle looks less attractive for application to manned space flight for the near future. The advantages of better range control and greater maneuverability after re-entry may eventually make this vehicle more desirable.

Propulsion

There has been much discussion of the relative merits of developing a larger booster engine or of clustering smaller ones. Both of these developments are required.

Schedule studies clearly indicate that a booster of one million pounds thrust or more could be available about three years earlier if it were based on the clustering of existing rocket engines. This would lead to a fourth generation of space vehicles (with Vanguard-Jupiter C being the first; IRBM-boosted space vehicles being the second; ICBM-boosted vehicles the third generation.) Progress in the rocket engine field offers a high degree of confidence that a multiple-barrel booster of one to one and a half million pounds total thrust could be ready for flight test in two to three years. Fifth-generation boosters based on the one million pounds-plus thrust, single-barrel engine (whether using one such engine or several) would offer orbital payloads up to 100,000 pounds, and would be available three years later.

It is strongly recommended that a study be made to assess the advisability of developing recoverable first-stage boosters. Recovery techniques should be optimized from a systems point of view.

Strong research effort on novel propulsion systems for vacuum operations is urged, and development of high-energy-propellant systems for upper stages should receive full support.

Vehicles for Early Experiments

In the preceding section several generations of space vehicle boosters are identified in general terms. The first generation, already in being, is capable of putting into orbit payloads of approximately 30 pounds. Such a vehicle enables the observation of a relatively small number of space environmental factors, or the conduct of simple experiments in the space environment. The second generation, with payload capabilities up to roughly 300 pounds, enables more sophisticated or larger numbers of experiments and environmental observations. The third-generation vehicles should make possible payloads of 3,000 pounds or more. Heavy or bulky observing instruments with provision for long-time attitude control and data transmission can be carried, and minimal manned space flights should be possible.

In each of these generations a number of boosters and upper stages are either available or under development. Proper combinations of these should make possible a wide spectrum of payloads and performances. Furthermore, it is likely that early generation vehicles will continue to be used even after later generation vehicles are available. Therefore the NASA should make a thorough study of the capabilities of existing stages to determine whether there are any serious gaps in the spectrum, and to select particular combinations for further development and use in its early experiments. With properly selective effort going into the early generations, a more vigorous development program for later generations of boosters and vehicles should be possible.

CONCLUSION

Scientific advances of the broadest import can result from substantially improved understanding of cosmic processes and their influence upon the environment, and therefore the inhabitants, of the earth. The acquisition of such understanding depends critically upon the establishment of observational vantage points outside the insulation of the earth's atmosphere. The discussions and suggestions regarding research policies, procedures and programs presented in this report are intended to further the rapid and efficient development of the requisite space flight capabilities. All of these suggestions include recommendations, either stated or implicit, for cooperation or close coordination with related work by other civil and military agencies. More detailed discussions and program recommendations in particular fields are treated by the Working Group reports.

APPENDIX

The Special Committee on Space Technology was established early in 1958 to advise the NACA regarding the development of its space research activities. The first meeting was held in the NACA Headquarters on February 13, 1958, with all members attending. The members:

Dr. H. Guyford Stever, Chairman
Colonel Norman C. Appold
Mr. Abraham Hyatt
Dr. Wernher von Braun
Dr. Hugh L. Dryden
Mr. Robert R. Gilruth
Mr. H. Julian Allen
Mr. Abe Silverstein
Dr. H. W. Bode

Dr. Milton U. Clauser
Professor Dale R. Corson
Mr. J. R. Dempsey
Mr. S. K. Hoffman
Dr. W. Randolph Lovelace, II
Dr. W. H. Pickering
Dr. Louis N. Ridenour
Dr. J. A. Van Allen
Mr. Carl B. Palmer, Secretary

The first task undertaken by the Committee was the development of a balanced, national civil space research program. To obtain the broad background in space science and technology required for such a project, a number of ad hoc Working Groups were appointed to consider particular aspects of space research. These groups were made up of individuals of recognized ability and experience and were headed by members of the Committee. This report was prepared in the light of the advice of these Working Groups and the NACA Committees on Aircraft, Missile, and Spacecraft Aerodynamics, Construction, and Propulsion.

The Working Groups and their composition:

1. Working Group on Space Research Objectives

Dr. J.A. Van Allen, Chairman
Professor Dale R. Corson
Colonel Norman C. Appold
Mr. Robert Cornog

Mr. Robert P. Haviland
Dr. J. R. Pierce
Professor Lyman Spitzer, Jr.
Mr. E. O. Pearson, Secretary

2. Working Goup on Vehicular Program

Dr. Wernher von Braun, Chairman
Mr. S. K. Hoffman
Colonel Norman C. Appold
Mr. Abraham Hyatt
Dr. Louis N. Ridenour
Mr. Abe Silverstein

Dr. Krafft A. Ehricke
Mr. M. W. Hunter
Mr. C. C. Ross
Dr. Homer J. Stewart
Mr. George S. Trimble, Jr.
Mr. William H. Woodward, Secretary

Appendix - 2

3. Working Group on Re-Entry

Dr. Milton U. Clauser, Chairman Mr. Harlowe J. Longfelder
Mr. H. Julian Allen Dr. J. C. McDonald
Mr. Mac C. Adams Professor S. A. Schaaf
Dr. Alfred J. Eggers, Jr. Colonel John P. Stapp
Mr. Maxime A. Faget Mr. R. Fabian Goranson, Secretary
Dr. A. H. Flax Mr. Harvey H. Brown, Secretary
Professor Lester Lees

4. Working Group on Range, Launch, and Tracking Facilities

Mr. J. R. Dempsey, Chairman Commander Robert F. Freitag
Mr. Robert R. Gilruth Professor J. Allen Hynek
Colonel Paul T. Cooper Mr. John T. Mengel
Mr. L. G. deBey Mr. Grayson Merrill
Mr. Carl E. Duckett Mr. Carl B. Palmer, Secretary

5. Working Group on Instrumentation

Dr. W. H. Pickering, Chairman Dr. Albert C. Hall
Dr. Louis N. Ridenour Mr. Eberhardt Rechtin
Dr. H. W. Bode Mr. William T. Russell
Mr. Robert W. Buchheim Dr. Robert C. Seamans, Jr.
Mr. Harry J. Goett Mr. Bernard Maggin, Secretary

6. Working Group on Space Surveillance

Dr. H. W. Bode, Chairman Mr. K. G. Macleish
Dr. W. H. Pickering Mr. William B. McLean
Mr. Wilbur B. Davenport, Jr. Mr. Alan H. Shapley
Mr. W. B. Hebenstreit Dr. Fred L. Whipple
Mr. Richard S. Leghorn Mr. Carl B. Palmer, Secretary

7. Working Group on Human Factors and Training

Dr. W. Randolph Lovelace, II, Colonel Edward B. Giller
  Chairman Dr. James D. Hardy
Mr. A. Scott Crossfield Mr. Wright Haskell Langham
Mr. Hubert M. Drake Dr. Ulrich C. Luft
Brig. General Donald D. Flickinger Mr. Boyd C. Myers, II, Secretary

www.ingramcontent.com/pod-product-compliance
Lightning Source LLC
Chambersburg PA
CBHW080516110426

42742CB00017B/3133